EAGLESHAM - AN EARL'S CREATION

EAGLESHAM

AN EARL'S CREATION

JANE SCOTT DEIGHTON

JOHNSON

LONDON

First published 1974

ISBN 0 85307 127 6
MADE AND PRINTED IN GREAT BRITAIN
BY CLARKE, DOBLE AND BRENDON LIMITED
FOR JOHNSON PUBLICATIONS LIMITED
11/14 STANHOPE MEWS WEST, LONDON, S.W.7

CONTENTS

ILLUSTRATIONS

❦

and

numerous line drawings

ACKNOWLEDGEMENTS

Thanks are due to many for the making of this book, especially the residents and business people of Eaglesham who have willingly shown me their properties and told me their tales, allowing me to make use of them in text and illustration.

Special mention must be made of Mrs. Jean Gardner for executing the line drawings, Miss Sheila Neilson for her photography of present-day scenes, Messrs. Henry, Downing and Prosser as well as Mrs. Christina Robertson Brown for supplying photographs of old Eaglesham and Cathcart, Rev. A. M. Bennett, B.D., for extracts from Parish Church Communicants' Roll Book, and also to Mrs. Jennifer Harris for typing the manuscript.

Perhaps most thanks are due to Dr. Donald Johnson, who encouraged me to write the book and generously published it.

I should like to record my thanks to them all and to my own family and friends for their great longsuffering.

PREFACE

by EDWARD TAYLOR, M.P.

〜⚭〜

Eaglesham—the village in Renfrewshire which is the subject of this book—is one of the most enchanting and delightful places in the West of Scotland. Although it is only a 15 minute journey by car from the boundary of the city of Glasgow, the quiet and peaceful atmosphere of Eaglesham seems like a different world from the hustle and bustle of an industrial city.

But the village is no museum piece. Although the houses strung along the two main streets on either side of the large grassy area have been carefully and painstakingly preserved, Eaglesham is a lively and vigorous community.

It must cause real discomfort to the twentieth century planners who have used all the skills and techniques of today to build new communities that the stresses, the strains and the problems which so regularly stem from modern social engineering have been overcome in this village which was planned by a Scottish nobleman in the eighteenth century.

But what is so special about Eaglesham? Why has it the qualities which made it a holiday resort in the last century and a place where the City dwellers come to capture a glimpse of tranquillity in the summer evenings or the winter weekends? Perhaps it is because with the large common parkland between the main streets, the atmosphere can never be dominated by the motor car. Perhaps it's because no giant factory dominates it. Perhaps it's because the main traffic arteries to the South and the West by-pass it. Perhaps it's because the main streets rise together on a hill which enables the visitor to stand at the top of the hill and see the whole village before him. Perhaps it's because the grim and wild moorland and hills of Renfrewshire adjoin the village. Or perhaps it's because the village is steeped in the history of Scotland and its people.

9

But one thing is certain—the village of Eaglesham has a magic which is all its own.

The time is long overdue to have a book about Eaglesham—its history and its people. But so often the works of history are dull and lifeless manuscripts because they do not capture and embrace the fact that towns and villages are places where real people live out their lives and face all the joys and sorrows of mortal life. Jane Scott Deighton's book happily overcomes this problem by weaving through the story of Eaglesham the story of a family which comes to live in the village and then moves on.

My only quarrel with the theme, as a lifelong resident in Cathcart, which has its own magic, its own history and its own pride of community is that Eaglesham is presented as a place where Tom and his young family came to as a refuge from Cathcart!

However, the delights of the book should overcome even these parochial complaints and I know that the readers of Jane Deighton's book will find themselves captivated by the charm of the village of Eaglesham and whet their appetites to join the many who visit the village and delight in it.

Chapter 1

BESTOWAL

In 1912 a Glasgow apprentice slater finished "serving his time" in his father's building firm and left home for Australia. Shortly after his arrival in Sydney he was befriended by an Australian family who had relations living in a country town, Orange.

During the course of a visit to grandparents, one of these "country cousins" became acquainted with the Glasgow man. The quiet, thoughtful young woman slowly responded to the dynamic influence of the Scotsman's personality and before long his proud boast that he would win her hand in marriage became an accomplished fact.

As a help to the young couple, her grandfather provided them with a house and in due course they started a family, with a daughter followed a couple of years later with another. They were beginning to feel a strain on their finances when the babes grew into toddlers and things became a little difficult on the slender budget.

A large section of the so-called civilised world was at war with another section, considered equally civilised. The young father enlisted in the Australian army and his wife had to manage alone, like countless others of her generation.

Eventually, peace was restored and the family settled back to normal living. Soon it became evident that a third child was on the way and they both knew things would become harder as a result.

In Scotland things were different. The economy was picking up after the First World War and among those reaping the benefit were all who belonged to the building industry. Letters reaching the little home in Sydney told how the slater brothers and their father were building up a first-class business and how their respective families were thriving.

Eventually a letter arrived from the Scots father himself, suggesting that his son return to Scotland with his Australian wife and children and enter the family business as a partner. He also promised to foot the bill for their voyage.

It did not take long for the impetuous young man to wind up all his affairs and uproot his wife and young daughters as well as his months-old son. Nor did it take long for his brothers to convince him, after a brief time back in Glasgow, that he was not wanted in the business.

Houses were very difficult to obtain and no more help on the financial side was forthcoming, so the family from Australia were hard pressed to find accommodation. For a time they shared rooms in a Cathcart tenement but later managed to find a little place on their own in the village of Eaglesham.

The young wife was captivated by the Renfrewshire village and soon set about learning its history. Between performing the usual duties of wife and mother she quietly, but persistently, gathered pieces of interesting information about the new environment into which she had come.

She was entranced at the antiquity of the village itself, delighted at learning that the land on which it was built was part of the dowry of a nobleman's daughter many centuries before, and utterly fascinated by the stories of the ancient family who had owned it all.

*   *   *

"We haven't much further to go now, Ei."

The slightly built woman sitting between her two young daughters in the back of the big black hired saloon motor car, smiled at her husband as he turned and spoke to her from his seat beside the driver.

"That's fine, because I think these girls are almost asleep—like Billy on your knee there." The little quiet laugh she gave was drowned instantly by her elder daughter's emphatic tones.

"I'm not sleepy at all, Mummy. I've been looking at all the different kinds of houses we have passed on the road."

"Good for you, Jane. That's the way to learn about things, by using your eyes." The curly-haired child settled more comfortably back into the seat, obviously pleased at receiving her father's approval.

"Sorry, dear. I thought you were nodding off when all the time you were looking out of the window and watching what there was to see." The young mother reached out her hand and ruffled the tousled curls affectionately.

"I'm looking for the great big green to play games on," piped up a tired little voice.

"Keep looking, Anna, because we are just coming to Eaglesham now and the green is right in the middle of it," her father assured her.

Even as he spoke, the car drove past a row of dwelling houses and entered a village community, which seemed to the watchful eyes of the occupants in the rear seat to be overshadowed by the large expanse of green in its centre.

"I think it's funny to see a paddock in among streets," and the tone of Jane's voice underlined her words.

"Is that the big field where we can play, Daddy?"

"That's it, Anna. Plenty of room for you to enjoy yourself there. Don't call it a field, though, or a paddock either because the people who live here think of it as a special possession. I've heard the name they give it, but can't remember what it is."

"It's called 'The Orry'," the driver supplied in an undertone.

"That's right. I seem to remember vaguely that the village belonged to some Lord or Earl at one time or another and that he wouldn't allow houses to be built on the big green. Do you know if that's correct?"

"The place has a long history, but I'm sorry I do not know any of the facts."

"I wonder if it did really belong to a titled gentleman?"

"Very possibly. Don't sound so awed though, Ei; titles are not as scarce here as in Australia. That's where my wife comes from," he added for the driver's information.

"Perhaps I'll find out sometime. It looks an attractive little place, Tom—much better than dirty, smokey Glasgow, and Cathcart, too, for that matter."

"It should be better for the children, at least."

The motor changed direction and started to climb gradually uphill, keeping the green common on its right. On the left they passed a neat stone church surrounded by a small graveyard, then travelled upwards passing little houses, cottages, shops and some larger houses.

Soon the driver steered the vehicle in to the edge of the narrow pavement and Eileen noticed how big the motor seemed beside the low roofed house with the small window frames, outside which it had stopped.

Her husband stepped out, still carrying the sleeping baby in his arms, and walked over to a small green-painted door. As she studied the buildings she thought how old and shabby some of them looked, yet here and there were signs of definite care. Because of the slope of the street, some of the window ledges were almost level with the roadway. Her husband's large frame practically filled the doorway where he stood and the guttering of the roof was no more than a couple of feet above his head.

As she watched, the door was opened by a stout woman who seemed to have been watching or waiting for his arrival. The woman gave Tom a curt nod as she handed over a key, then started to direct him further up the hill. After a brief discussion, he returned to the waiting occupants of the car.

"Is that our new house, Mummy?" little Anna was having difficulty in keeping her eyes open.

"We're just going up the road to it right now. Off we go, driver, to the Wallace's new abode." Tom turned round and gave his younger daughter a playful wink. "Anna is longing for her bed."

Eileen watched her husband's expression and could tell from it that he was glad to be away from the Cathcart "digs". She wondered if they would be able to stay in this new place for any length of time. They seemed to have been shuttling from pillar to post since ever they had stepped from the liner which carried them across the world from her own sunny Australia.

She glanced from him to the scene itself; it certainly was very different to their previous place. Instead of looking across the road at a rather muddy river, with pieces of dead trees and an assortment of refuse defiling it, she saw only lovely green grass and a great number of trees, just beginning to burst into leaf. She loved the greenness of the grass in Scotland.

Suddenly the car stopped before a closed wooden door, surmounted by an ornate overhang with side pieces, which she took to be the entrance to her new residence. She was surprised, therefore, when the

14

driver carried their baggage through a narrow gap between two gable
ends of grey stone buildings, and disappeared from view.

"Why don't we go in by the door on the front street?"

"Because that leads to the downstairs houses."

"Is ours the upstairs house, then?"

"Well, it is one of them, anyway."

Eileen sustained a second shock as she grasped the situation. What
she had supposed to be the house which Tom had found them, was, in
fact, several houses.

*   *   *

It didn't take the little family very long to find its feet in the new
environment. Eileen had experienced a few qualms on first sight of the
two small rooms which she had approached by an outside stone stairway. The nearness of the other occupants of the "upstairs houses"
likewise caused her some misgivings.

However, the serenity of the situation, with its view of the trees and
grass on the common from the front window, and the tidy garden and
washing greens stretching far up from the back of the building, compensated fairly adequately.

Jane had been admitted to the village school and had already made
friends with one or two of the village children. A child from one of the
houses nearby had taken a strong liking to Anna and took her to play
by the hour on the grassy slopes of the Orry, as the common was
referred to by the local inhabitants. Even the baby knew a change.
Instead of his erstwhile constant crying, he now lay quite contentedly
on a high-backed sofa facing the front window and kicked and gurgled
baby noises at the trees outside.

Eileen had no bother whatsoever in carrying out all the routine duties
of the average wife and mother, yet still found time to read up old
volumes of Scottish history in quest of information about the origins
of the place where she now lived.

In chance conversations with people who had lived in Eaglesham all
their lives, and some of their forebears before them, she gradually
pieced the story together in something of a skeleton form.

They could all tell her of the family of noble birth to whom the
entire area, as well as Eaglesham, belonged. She learned that Eglinton
was their title and their actual family name was Montgomery. Thus the
street in which she lived derived it name.

15

One evening, when the three children were sleeping snugly and soundly in the little front room, Tom told her he had been speaking to an old man in Glasgow that forenoon.

"He has been coming to Eaglesham for his summer holidays for years now."

"You really mean that some people think on this little place as a holiday spot?" Eileen couldn't quite manage to keep the amusement out of her tone.

"Of course they do. Lots of them. What's wrong with that?"

"There's no sea or beach." It was as simple as that.

"This isn't Sydney, Eileen. You forget."

"I'll never do that, I can assure you."

The sharpness of tone was unusual for her, she knew, but he had touched her on the raw. How often, in fact, she remembered every tiny detail of their wonderful holidays spent in the sun on the golden stretches of beach with the rolling surf pounding the sand nearby.

"Well, anyway, lots of people enjoy summer holidays here, believe it or not."

"I suppose in comparison to the awful tenement closes, with their dunnies and back courts, and the way their poor children are brought up, this place will seem like Paradise."

"More or less," and she detected a hint of resentment in his voice. Tom didn't like her to poke fun at his home land and she had to admit inwardly that she didn't like it when anyone did so at her beloved Australia. Still, there really was no comparison between the two, but she had better not voice that opinion at the moment, she decided.

"I'm sorry to have interrupted you. What were you going to say about this old man?"

"As I said already, he has been coming here every summer for a long time and he's been trying to find out all he can about this place. I thought you would like to meet him, so I've told him to come and see us some time."

"Oh, that's a good idea. Perhaps he will be able to tell me about the things and people I've been wondering about."

"You certainly seem to find this wee village very interesting."

"I certainly do. I think it's amazing that it was built before Captain Cook even discovered Australia—and think how different Aussie is since that time, yet this little place has stayed virtually the same as it

16

1. Royal Oak Inn in Montgomery Street

EAGLESHAM 'BUS.

[Published by W. Prosser, Supply Stores, Cathcart.

2.   Eaglesham Horsedrawn Bus at Clarkston

was in the days when the Earl himself saw it taking shape according to his plan."

"Oh, my word. You sound quite knowledgeable. You have discovered who it was that the village belonged to, I take it."

"Oh, yes. As well as a lot more." She laughed lightheartedly. "It's all so interesting and every other day I learn another little bit of information to add to my store. I find it all great fun."

Tom sat silently watching her.

She began to feel uneasy with his steady gaze fixed on her face for so long.

"What's the matter. Are you annoyed at me?"

Her question surprised him into instant alertness.

"Good gracious, no. Why should I be?"

"You looked as though you didn't approve of my interest in the past of this place. Or don't you think I should concern myself with such people as Earls and the like?"

"I wasn't thinking anything like that at all, I'll assure you."

"But you were thinking something."

"Admittedly." He smiled, and she wondered whether it meant he was amused or pleased. Even after about ten years of marriage to him, she was never quite certain how to interpret his moods or reactions.

"I was thinking how unusual it must be for a woman like yourself to spend her spare time, and her imagination, on things like that. Somehow, I always thought womenfolk only liked talking and thinking about domestic affairs, or fancy clothes."

She must have registered a mild form of indignation at the remark, for he followed it up with a quiet chuckle.

"That is, as well as talking about their neighbours."

She really did show her indignation at that.

"That's one thing I won't let you away with, Tom."

"Don't get angry, my dear. I'm not accusing you of such petty thoughts. I merely said that I had always thought of women in that light—till I met you."

"Now you're just trying to wriggle out." She did not know whether to be angry or amused, now.

"I am not. I really mean it. I have always believed you are a wonderful wee woman, far above your kind."

"Stop kidding. Anyone would think you were an Irish man, come straight from kissing the Blarney."

"What do you know about the Blarney stone. I am the one with Irish blood running through my veins, not you."

"That's all you know."

"You've told me often that your mother's people came originally from England and your father's from Wales," he grinned broadly, as though pleased at being able to remind her of the facts.

"Ah, yes, but did I never tell you that Mum's grandmother came from Sligo?"

"Perhaps you did. I'm not interested in her, though. You are the one who interests me. Tell me how you dug up this information you spoke of."

Although the spring had given way to summer, the evenings still had a little chill to them. A mixture of coal and small logs burned in the gleaming kitchen range and Tom instinctively drew his chair a little closer to its warmth.

"It does get chilly here in the evenings."

Eileen followed his lead and made herself more comfortable in an easy chair, covered in dark green velvet which had seen better days.

"I really just listened to everything which everybody told me about Eaglesham and its past owners, then wrote it all down in a notebook." She supposed that her husband would think she was stupid in spending her time thus.

"I did visit one of the public libraries and read up some history books, to fit in the bits which were missing."

"History books?" Tom's expression was a study.

"Yes, that's right." Her answer did nothing to dispel the utter amazement registered on his face.

"History books are only for school children."

"Oh, well, since I never attended school in my life that is the reason I must read them now."

"You must have been to school sometime, Ei."

It was her turn to give him an answering look of amazement.

"How do you think I could ever have attended school, living miles from anywhere on the big sheep farm as I did when I was a girl?"

"Right enough! Do you know, I never even thought about it. Did none of you go to school, then?" She had to smile at the incredulity of his tone.

"Only Blanche. And that was because she was determined to have an education and become a teacher herself. She had to leave home and go to school in the town."

"How did the rest of you learn anything?"

"Fortunately for us, both Mum and Dad had been well educated. They were our teachers."

"It's as well for you that your parents could do so."

"I'm sure there are plenty of Australians of my age whose people did not have any proper schooling. They seem to manage well enough, in spite of everything."

"You quite enjoyed reading these history books, did you?"

"I found them very enlightening, anyway. You must remember that I had only heard of Scotland, and not much more, when I came here. I certainly knew nothing of her past. The books taught me a lot, but I realise that there must be very much more still to learn. For such a tiny country, it has a wealth of intriguing history."

"Has it? I don't remember very much about history. Maybe I didn't listen to my teacher in my school days. I don't think all that stuff that happened long ago, matters to us nowadays."

"I think we are what we are, because of what happened long ago. Surely the present is always shaped by the past, in any age or any country?"

"Do you really think so? I wonder!"

"I do think so, Tom. The more I read, the more I discover that to be true."

"You are a dark horse, aren't you? When did you do all this reading and writing? I haven't seen you at it."

She had to laugh at his masculine arrogance, though she was certain that he didn't have the faintest idea he was being arrogant.

"Mostly when you were at your work, in the afternoons."

"I would like to read this manuscript, scribe-wife."

"Now you are laughing at me."

"No, I'm not. I think you are a wonder, finding time to do it when you have three youngsters to look after and the usual amount of work that goes with a young family."

"Oh, there's not much housework to be done here. Things keep so much cleaner in this air than they did in Glasgow. I do have some mending to do now, though. Jane was playing with some chums in the Orry on the way home from school and fell headlong on the Mid Road.

She's made a great hole in her school jersey which will need to be repaired for the morning."

"Fetch me your notebook, first, and I'll read your story while you are darning the jersey."

She felt sure that he was mocking her and pretended not to hear him, but he wouldn't be put off. In the long run, she reluctantly produced the cheap notebook she had bought from Dalgleish's store.

"Now for a dip into the past." She watched him for a moment as he settled down deeper into his chair before the dancing flames in the old range, then went off in search of the school jersey needing repairing.

The handwriting in the notebook was sadly back-hand, but fairly legible in spite of it, and Tom had no difficulty in reading.

The narrative started by stating that a legend existed which affirmed that the family of Montgomerie, who were the owners of Eaglesham, originated in Roman times. As there did not appear to be any valid proof of it, though, Eileen preferred to disregard the tale and start from as far back as she could trace. He read on:

* * *

Renfrewshire formed part of the ancient Kingdom of Strathclyde (which stretched from Cumberland in the north of England to the River Clyde in central Scotland) and possessed a history of bloody battles and changing loyalties. It claimed great importance in the story of Scotland's past because within its confines many important events took place, among them the beginnings of the Royal House of Stewart.

The owners of this part where we now live were closely connected to the highest in the land and played a prominent role in Scotland's history.

By the time of the reign of King Malcolm III Scotland was a united country, covering almost the same area as it does now; Vikings, who had invaded and settled in the off-shore islands to the north, were in control of them, but the rest of the country was under the king's supreme command, which fact earned him the title of Canmore, meaning Great Head. During his reign other men of Viking descent, Normans from the French coast, crossed the narrow English Channel and successfully invaded England. Under their leader, William, Duke of Normandy, they landed with an army on the 28th September 1066, on the South Coast of England—with every intention of conquering the island. On

20

14th October of the same year a fierce battle was fought between the Duke's forces and those of the English King, Harold, at a place on the coast called Hastings. After one whole day's fighting, William gained a decisive victory; Harold and his best men lost their lives. On Christmas Day 1066 the Norman William (thereafter referred to always as William the Conqueror) had himself crowned King of England, in London's Westminster Abbey.

When William crossed the Channel from Normandy he was accompanied by many Norman noblemen, among them Roger de Montgomerie, Viscounte de Hiesmes. This man was said to be cousin german to Robert, Duke of Normandy (William's father) and he commanded the van of the Normandy Army at the Battle of Hastings.

In return for his good services, William exalted him to the dignity of Earl of Arundel and Shrewsbury, granting him most extensive territory in the south and west of England, particularly in Shropshire, and bestowing on him the Castle of Arundel.

The sweet fruit of success seemed to spur this man on to attempt his own personal conquest, of Wales instead of England, and part of that country retains his interest in it even yet, in a shire bearing his name. The famous Doomsday Book records that he owned 150 castles in England and Wales, so he must have been a very successful as well as a very ambitious man. (Montgomeryshire is where Grandfather Bowen lived before he left Wales for Australia, I remember him telling me.)

Harold's son Edgar, the Saxon heir, had to flee with his family from the Normans and travelled by sea to Fife in Scotland. These refugees were welcomed by Scotland's King Malcolm to his capital, the town of Dunfermline, also in Fife. Eventually Edgar's sister, Margaret, became Malcolm's queen, after the death of his first wife Ingibiorg, and brought about many beneficial changes in her husband's kingdom. The King was killed during an attack against Rufus' forces at Alnwick in the North of England in 1093, and on hearing the news of his death, his queen died in Edinburgh. After their deaths their younger children were sent away to be brought up in England, where their son David, going to the court of William Rufus, became both scholar and knight. He succeeded his father as King of Scotland in 1124 and when he came north to take the throne he brought with him some of the Normans to penetrate Scotland without a military conquest. Many families from across the English Channel found their way into Scotland at that time.

21

As King David already held very extensive estates in the English midlands, he had many ready-made knight tenants for his newer Scottish estates. The King was a generous patron and many from far-off fields benefited by his patronage.

One such was Walter from Shropshire, younger son of a Breton named Alan, son of Flaald, from Dol in Brittany, who had been very favoured by England's King Henry, son of William the Conqueror. (This Walter Fitz Alan (son of Alan) was Fleance of Shakespeare's Macbeth.) He joined King David's service about 1136 and was made the chief officer of the royal household, thus becoming the first High Steward (Stewart) of Scotland or High Constable of Scotland. As such, he was given the lordships of Renfrew, Paisley, Eaglesham and North Kyle in Ayrshire, becoming tenant-in-chief of that area to the King, swearing to obey him and bring a fixed number of knights to fight for him when required.

When Walter and Eschina, his wife, came north to Scotland they brought with them a host of other Norman, Breton and Flemish settlers with their knights, archers, servants and womenfolk. These all made themselves comfortable in Renfrewshire and Ayrshire, areas of the west of Scotland. Just as the King granted office and land to his followers in return for knightly services, so these in turn bestowed smaller areas or fiefs to their own followers, many of which were also held by military service. Thus the invading Normans who entered England came to Scotland as conquerors, by invitation of her King. In this way feudalism was introduced to Scotland, and the Normans became the new landed aristocracy—lording it over the native peoples who had to work for them as serfs. In 1157 Malcolm IV, confirming the grant previously made by King David I, bestowed Renfrew Castle and lands on Walter FitzAlan.

One of the nobles who accompanied Walter FitzAlan from Wales was Robert de Mondegumbri (Montgomerie), a grandson of Roger de Montgomerie, Earl of Arundel and Shrewsbury (referred to previously). Walter conferred the Manor and lands of Eaglesham (a spelling shown in 1158 was Egilsham) on Robert, as the dowry of his daughter Marjory whom Robert espoused as his first wife. Hence he became the first Lord of Eaglesham and his name appears as witness to the endowment made by Walter FitzAlan, of the present 900-year-old Paisley Abbey which is sometimes called Scotland's Westminster.

At the time of its bestowal on Robert de Montgomerie, Eaglesham was probably little more than a group of primitive dwellings with, possibly, its own small church. The land of a lord, or sub-tenant, was known as his domain and the country was divided into areas called parishes, which corresponded in size to the lord's domain. Each hamlet or village, as these groups of homes were called, became subject to its own lord and the men of them had often to perform certain duties for their lord, in return for the lands they held. Some were free; but many were serfs who had to wear iron collars which showed what, and whose, they were.

Some local folk think that Eaglesham derived its name from the fact of its having a Church, maintaining that it comes from the Celtic word *eaglis* meaning church and the Saxon *ham* for village. Other interpretations are that it derives from the fact that eagles perched on the site prior to buildings being erected on it, or that it comes from "Ecclesiaholm" meaning the church in the hollow. Still another line of thought holds that it was, in fact, called after a man Egil or Egli (Egilsham of 1158 spelling, thus being Egli's village). Possibly any one of these interpretations could be correct but, like so many such things, the true origin is lost in antiquity.

One thing seems to be certain, though. The coming of these Normans, of Viking origin, and possessors of courageous, assertive and fearless character, brought a new spirit of adventure to the Scottish scene.

* * *

Tom put the book down and took a long look at his wife, sitting quietly plying darning wool and needle to his elder daughter's small jersey. She wondered what he thought of her work, but felt rather hesitant about enquiring. It had cost her quite a lot of time to gather the information and write it all down. More than that, she had become not a little attached to her task and was rather afraid of an unfavourable opinion, lest it spoiled her own enjoyment in it.

She need not have feared. He crossed over to where she sat with her darning and, stooping down, kissed her bent forehead with a murmured "I told you before that I think you're a great wee woman. Have I ever told you how proud I am to be your husband?"

Chapter 2

HERITAGE

Soon after settling into the new accommodation, Eileen set about acquiring as much knowledge of the village, and the people who had owned it, as she could. Much of what she gleaned by her enquiries locally proved to be of a repetitive nature, causing her to extend the scope of her queries. A helpful acquaintance lent her an old volume of the history of Renfrewshire which she found made engrossing reading. Many incidents in the history of the Montgomery family captivated her imagination, but perhaps the one which excelled all others was the account of the Battle of Otterburn in 1388, when Sir John Montgomery of Eglisham took Sir Henry Percy, son of the Earl of Northumberland, prisoner, and with the ransom so won built Polnoon Castle. She became so spellbound by the story that she determined to find the Castle, and, having done so, wrote a long letter to a sister in Australia relating all to her.

She also learned from the local residents that the village had a Covenanter connection and was shown the grave and memorial stone in the churchyard.

*   *   *

During the Glasgow "Fair Holiday" week the village had been a much busier place, with groups of boys and girls playing on the broad slopes of the Orry at all hours of the day, and youths and maidens playing different games well into the night. The water of the burn which ran through the Orry like a backbone, proved a major source of attraction to the city lads but their sisters seemed to prefer chalking "beds" for games of "peever" all over the village pavements.

Jane had been mystified with the execution of the latter when she first witnessed it, but the other girls hadn't taken very long to instruct her in the intricacies of drawing the diagram or "beds" with a piece of pipe clay, usually right in front of someone's doorway, and the method of hopping from one square into the next. She played happily at such games for hours on end and Anna was quite content to play an onlooker's part.

Only very occasionally was there any motor traffic on the roads, as most deliveries were still made by horsedrawn vans or carts, so the mothers of Eaglesham experienced little fear of accidents to their children.

After Tom resumed his work at the end of the holiday period, Eileen made the best of the long hours of daylight and the warmer weather, before Jane had to return to school. As soon as her husband left the little upstairs house and hurried down the outside stone staircase to catch the early morning bus which took him to his father's business in Glasgow's Eglinton Street, Eileen set to with energy and efficiency.

It was no effort to her to perform all the routine tasks involved in her tiny house, which was but a mere fraction of her household duties on her father's large farm and sheep station. When they were completed, she would make up a wholesome packed lunch for herself and the children, leave everything set out ready in the tidy kitchen for the evening meal, shut the door behind her and set off with her little brood for a day in the open countryside.

Sometimes she headed for the moor road to the west of the village and then climbed up Ballageich hill, leaving the baby's push-chair at the bottom. Both the girls enjoyed that, scrambling up the steep incline ahead of their mother, who found it hard going to climb with her bouncing boy fidgeting about in her arms. Sometimes she settled for a spot halfway up the hill, when they picnicked there and rested for a bit before finishing the climb. When she did attain the plateau above, she always felt it had been worth all the effort just to be able to gaze on the wonderful panorama which unfolded before her eyes. Moorland, mountain, loch and sea all combined to present a picture of Scotland

26

in miniature. If it was a really clear day she could discern the dome-shaped island resting in the wide estuary of the Clyde, which Tom had told her was called Ailsa Craig, but which his old Irish father had invariably referred to as "Paddy's Milestone" as it lay to the side of the route the ships sailed between Scotland and Ireland.

Other days she chose the old Strathaven road, walking down Montgomery Street to the Cross, then turning up Gilmour Street, passing the school and out into wide-open country with delightful green grass and healthy Ayrshire cattle contentedly enjoying it.

There she took the children into a quiet field where they ate their packed lunch before making the return journey.

Perhaps the children enjoyed most of all the days when she took them down the Glasgow road as far as Waterfoot. There was a certain secluded grassy hideaway which she had discovered on their first visit there. It was not far from the Lade, near the spot which somebody had told her was called "Horses' Drink", as the horses crossed from the Waterfoot Smithy to relieve their thirst in its clear water. It had proved a restful setting, that first time she enjoyed it, with the gentle lapping sound of the water and the cool shade of the leafy trees. The trees themselves were a constant source of delight to her; so different in their appearance to any of the varieties of gums with which she was familiar.

The old grain mill, with the row of little cottages nearby, lent a certain charm to the rural picture and the dancing waters of the clear, swift-flowing river which she knew was the White Cart in its pristine state, never failed to amaze her. So enchanting here, but not so very much further along its course it would lose its crystal appearance, and by the time it reached Cathcart it would bear no resemblance to the pure stream at her feet.

She often thought about the dirty, muddy river she had hated when she lived near it. Mud she was used to, but household rubbish of all shapes and sizes she had found objectionable. Not for a moment had she regretted her husband's choice of Eaglesham as a place for them to live. She allowed her imagination full rein as she sat on the soft grass, watching her children play at the water's edge. The sound of occasional motor vehicles and the clip-clop of horses' hooves, as they pulled the farm wagons along, fell on her ears.

Instead of the slow moving, lumbering farmers' drays or the noisy, wheezing motor cars driving along the road above where she sat, she fancied she heard different sounds.

In place of the hard-surfaced road she envisaged a well-trodden bridle path along the river bank. Fine specimens of horses, chestnut or darkest shining brown, carried equally fine specimens of riders on their strong backs. As they sped along, their tails and manes waving furiously as their mounts spurred them forward, she could almost feel her nostrils smart with the pungent stench from their hot flesh. So vivid were the portrayals of her imagination, that at times she found herself letting her body respond to the sway and the rhythm of the galloping hooves. Then she would tauten up as she drew rein, halting the powerful animal quickly to a standstill beside the shallow pool, to drink its fill before heading off again in the direction of Polnoon Castle where My Lord and My Lady awaited her arrival.

At other times, her imaginative mind would envisage the same road at a later date, by which time it had been changed from the bridle path to a wider dust road, bearing elegant coaches and carriages on its winding way. She let her thoughts conjure up images of wealthy men, with their ladies arrayed in gorgeous gowns and exquisite furs, riding past in handsome, shiny carriages drawn by groomed horses, on their way to attend a ball or formal entertainment in the castellated mansion house set in parkland high above where she sat. The name of it she knew to be Eaglesham House, but she preferred to think of it as the Castle, as all the Eaglesham folk did. When she shut her eyes and indulged in such daydreaming, she practically heard the clip-clop of the horses' hooves slow down as the driver negotiated the coach's turn through the pillared gateway and into the long drive on the last lap of its journey to the main entrance in front of the row of stately cypress trees. Inside the spacious home of the Gilmours, amid fine furnishings and tasteful surroundings, titled ladies and gentlemen of noble birth might rub shoulders with more newly-rich Glasgow merchants and industrialists, and their wives.

Although vivid, these reveries were always of the briefest nature, as one or other of the children would draw her attention to something of interest—in the much more realistic present.

Once or twice she had been joined on her walks, or part of them, by one of the natives of Eaglesham. Many had noted the newcomer and, after giving themselves time to take stock of her, and ascertain the reason for her insatiable interest in them and their village, were ready to be both friendly and helpful, whenever the opportunity presented itself.

Soon after she had come to live in the village, she had been buying groceries in one of the little shops. The elderly shopkeeper had been very talkative and wanted to know whether she had made Anna's dress herself. She had explained that her mother in Australia had made it and given it to the child before she left there. The older woman had been impressed to learn that the fair-haired child had been born not far from where a nephew of her own had settled in Sydney. From then onwards, whether in the shop or the village streets, Anna proved a source of interest to shopkeeper and shoppers alike. Her blonde, straight hair was often to be seen bobbing alongside the darker hair of one of Eaglesham's children. Sometimes the country of her children's, and her own, birth gave an older person the opportunity to speak.

On just one such occasion, Eileen pushed the baby in his go-chair up Gilmour Street towards the Cross, following the two girls who had gone on ahead to buy the home-made "Toffee Jeans" she had promised them if they were well behaved on the road home from their picnic at Waterfoot. An old man, whom she knew by sight only, approached her with a friendly smile.

"You are the Australian, lady, am I right?"

"Yes, I am an Australian." Somehow Eileen had never thought of herself as the only one around, but he made her sound as though she were.

"I see you taking your children out every day and mentioned to my wife—only this morning—that you seem to be a great one for your family."

Eileen tried not to appear surprised at his remarks, but found it hard to follow his reason for making the statement. Surely every mother was "a great one for her family" as he quaintly put it.

"So many village mothers just let the kiddies play round about the doors or in the Orry but you always seem to make time to go out with yours."

She laughed softly as she explained.

"I can assure you that I don't only do it for their sakes. My purpose is a bit selfish, really. I visit all the nearby places to satisfy my own curiosity and I couldn't leave the children to do so, so they are trailed along whether they wish it or not."

At that point, Jane and Anna returned, each clutching in her hand a poke, made from a curled piece of paper, and chewing happily.

"They don't look in any way unhappy about the state of things," and the old man laughed as he looked down at the two girls.

29

"What about your wee brother. Aren't you going to give him one of your sweeties?" he asked Jane.

"He's too little to eat toffees, Daddy says," piped up Anna.

"Mummy buys him a bar of chocolate in Dalgleish's," Jane told him shyly.

"Oh, so that's it. What about Mummy? What does she get?"

"She gets the dinner ready." Anna didn't see the old man turn his head aside to hide his broad grin at her reply, which was just as well, Eileen thought. She was a touchy little thing at times, and wouldn't have understood his humour.

"I really wanted to ask if you would like the loan of an old book which I have in the house. My wife tells me that you are very interested in Eaglesham's past."

"That's right. I am interested in its present too."

"Well, you can find out all about its present easily enough, but maybe you would like to read something which has been written about its past."

"I certainly would. In fact, I have been going around some of the libraries to find what I could about it. It intrigues me."

"Well, if you'll stop by my house, after you have bought your son his chocolate, I'll give you this old book. I will be watching for you coming out of the shop."

Without more fuss, the old man doffed his tweed cap and walked on ahead of them with a brisk step for his years.

Tom had told her that morning not to look for him before nine o'clock, as he expected to work late on the big contract which they had recently won.

The children were all tired with the fresh air, and the walk earlier, so as soon as she had given them their evening meal, Eileen bathed them quickly in the tin bath before the kitchen range, and settled them all down in the room at the front. Almost as soon as they were in their beds, they dropped off into sound sleep. With a deep feeling of contentment, she lifted the large book which the old man had lent her and settled down with it before the fire. Even though the weather was fairly warm through the day, she did appreciate the comfort of a fire in the evenings.

Although she had already learned some of the story behind the formation of Eaglesham, she read avidly all the facts presented in the book newly come into her hands. Much of it, in fact, she had shown her husband, written in the simple notebook in her own handwriting.

Certain incidents gripped her imagination more than others, but she found all of it engrossing. In the quiet, peaceful atmosphere of the little home in Montgomery Street, her fertile mind conjured up scenes which would have been enacted in the area centuries previously. Before putting the book away in a safe place for the time being, she had decided on the following day's outing. She would go in search of what was left of Polnoon Castle.

* * *

The next day dawned and the children were awake early with the bright sunlight.

"Are we going to have a picnic again today, Mummy?"

"Would you like that, Anna?"

"Yes. Jane, would you like a picnic again, Janey?" She tugged her sister's hand impatiently as she awaited her answer.

"Can we have lemonade at it again?"

"Perhaps we will have 'fizzy orange' today instead."

"Oh, yes please Mummy."

The baby had been lying quietly in his wooden cot but the noise of the girls' excited voices must have reached him and he demanded attention.

"Hurry up with your breakfast, then, both of you and I'll see to Billy."

The girls did as she had asked them, and within a very short time the little group descended the stone staircase at the back of the building and headed down the hill, past the Church and turned into Gilmour Street. As she passed the garage she overheard two housewives chatting at their doorways nearby.

"There's that Mrs. Wallace taking her kids away again."

"She's a queer one, isn't she?"

"I should think she is! What do you suppose she does after she leaves the village?"

"Well, I dunno. Mind you she does always have that big bag with her."

"P'rhaps she sells things . . . you know, like the gypsies."

"Do you think she does?"

"Never can tell with these foreigners, can you?"

Eileen felt her cheeks burn, but pretended she had not even heard them. Her anger was kindled, though, and her steps became very determined. As she walked on towards open countryside and headed for the old Strathaven road, she recalled the strong feelings of patriotism to the "Mother country" engendered in all of them by her parents. Now she was classed as a foreigner within its shores. That hurt.

At the signpost on the corner she turned sharp left and, before she had gone very far down the country road, she was met by half a dozen very healthy-looking Ayrshire cows coming towards her.

Anna drew close in to her skirt, but Jane laughed.

"It's like Uncle Maurice's farm, isn't it, Mummy?"

The mention of her brother in far-off Australia brought an unexpected lump to Eileen's throat; she thought again of the remark of the woman she had passed only a short time before. She supposed that in a way she really was a foreigner in these parts.

The cows were looking at them in a stupid fashion, not knowing whether to proceed or retreat.

Anna started to cry.

"It's all right, dear. They won't hurt you. They are more afraid of you than you are of them. Look!"

She walked towards the largest cow and spoke in a soothing tone. The big eyes studied her for a second, while the beast seemed to be wondering whether she were friend or foe, then the animal meekly allowed her to advance. Once beyond it, she had no difficulty in conducting her children safely past the other beasts.

"Will there be any more cows on the road, Mummy?"

"I don't think there will be, Anna, but there is nothing to worry about even if there are."

"I don't like them."

A little weatherbeaten woman had appeared on the roadway just ahead of them emerging from one of the cottages across from an old Mill.

She looked questioningly at them all in turn and when they drew level with her, addressed Eileen.

"Have you lost your way, dearie? Can I help you?"

"Thank you. I am on the right way to Polnoon Castle, am I?"

Eileen thought she could not have been more surprised if she had asked her if she was on the right way to the moon.

She studied Eileen closely, then had a better look at each of the children.

"Will you be on the look-out for a job, is that it?"

3.   Montgomery Street and the Green where Tom played as a bare-footed boy

4 Eaglesham Cotton Mill after the Fire

Now it was Eileen's turn to be surprised. Did she look like a servant girl, then? Was that it? Then the funny side of it dawned on her.

"I would have had to live a long time before now, to be able to find work in Polnoon Castle, would I not?" and she laughed, as she thought of how odd she must have sounded to this other woman.

After only a very brief hesitation, the older woman joined in the joke.

"Aye, you would that. It's a long, long time since anybody lived at Polnoon."

"I just really want to have a look at what is left of the old place. I come from a country which has no castles, or any old buildings at all, you see."

"You are an American, are you?"

"I am Australian."

"My! Fancy that! How ever did you get here?"

The old woman was even more amazed this time.

"By ship," Eileen couldn't resist replying.

"I mean, what made you come to a wee country place like this?"

In no time at all, a conversation was well under way between the two, with the old woman listening intently and rubbing at her eyes with worn hands, as though making sure she were not dreaming.

Eileen told how she had married a Scotsman over in Australia and set up home, in the Bankstown area of Sydney, where they had two daughters and were expecting their third child.

"I was as happy as any young wife and mother could be. I had a comfortable house and my husband had a secure job, both of which were linked to the tannery and boot-making business which my grandfather owned."

"That would all be quite different to this place." The little woman looked about her, firstly at the surrounding green fields, then the old mill buildings and ultimately towards the houses across from the mill.

"It was."

"Come away into my place and I'll make you a wee cup of tea before you go walking any further."

Eileen would have remonstrated, but sensed that she would be hurting the other's feelings had she done so.

"Are you not on your way to the village?" was all she said.

"There's no hurry. I've all day long to get there and back," and she bustled off ahead of them in the direction of her house.

"Come on, bairnies. Bring your Mammy in to see Old Grannie and you'll get a drink of milk."

Eileen started to push the baby's go-chair in the direction of the woman's progress, but then saw that Jane remained firmly where she was, holding her little sister back with a tight grip on her hand which the younger child tried to release.

"Come on, Janey. Mummy is going to visit the old lady. Old Grannie, she is."

"She's not our Grannie." As she spoke Jane gave her sister's hand a defiant tug.

"She said Old Grannie."

"Well, we haven't any Grannie. We've got a Grandma here in Scotland and a Gran in Australia, so we can't have a Grannie here, too."

Eileen had to stop herself smiling at the child's reasoning.

"Come on, girls. Let's give the little old lady a visit. I think she is probably lonely."

"I don't like old ladies."

"You'll be an old lady yourself some day, Jane."

"I won't. I'll be just like you—always."

After a bit of cajoling, she managed to persuade Jane that no harm would come to her. Together the little group entered the doorway through which the small bent form had gone.

Eileen saw Jane's face suddenly light up and when she followed the direction of the girl's eyes, into a far corner of the little cottage kitchen, she saw what had caused it. Three tiny brown and white puppies playfully jumped around their mother.

All fear of contact with "Old Grannie" seemed to vanish in an instant. Within seconds, both the girls were standing near the dogs and laughing happily at the antics of the smallest pup. Even Billy jumped excitedly up and down on her knee as he watched them.

"Do you like doggies?" The question was asked as the woman handed Jane a large glass of creamy milk.

For a moment only, the child hesitated. Then she reached out for the milk and answered as she took it.

"Yes. I love them. Thank you for the milk . . . Grannie."

Before Eileen had time to be surprised at her daughter's reversal of opinion, Anna's high voice piped out.

"You said she wasn't our Grannie."

"I'm just everybody's Grannie. All the children hereabout call me

Old Grannie. There's always one or other of the Millhall bairns in, seeing old Betsy here and her pups."

As the two women shared a pot of tea, and the children sat on a hand-plaited rug on the floor, watching the dogs, Eileen told Old Grannie more about herself and how she had come to stay in Eaglesham.

"What made you ask about Polnoon Castle?"

"I have been learning all about the Earls and people who used to live there, and thought I would like to see what's left of it for myself."

"I don't know about any Earl or such like ever living there. It's always been just an old riddle o' stones."

It was very obvious she didn't think it had ever been anything else. No one could have told her about Otterburn.

"Folks think any old-like place with thick walls must have been a palace or a castle or some such. What would anybody want building a castle in a place like this? Take my word for it, Polnoon Castle was probably just an old house, maybe a bit bigger and better built than any of the others hereabout. People today call the big house down the Glasgow road 'Eaglesham Castle'."

"I think I'll still have a look at what remains, just the same. Is it very far from here?"

She didn't want to offend the old lady by telling her that she knew there had been a real Polnoon Castle. Instead, she took her leave and thanked her for her tea and kindness, in the pleasantest manner she knew.

"You are welcome, my dear. I'm all on my own nowadays and it's good to have a crack with a new face, I can tell you. Come and see me again soon. Come on out to the front now and I'll show you where to go."

As they did so, Eileen commented on the lay-out of the houses. She had not seen any cottages built in quite the same manner anywhere else. The main part of the building faced the roadway, which ran past the mill itself, before crossing the river. Other little houses were built on to it at right angles on each end, forming a broad U-shape forecourt.

"They were built for the workers in the Mill there."

"It's a lovely spot to stay in, with all the trees and fields right on your doorstep."

"Is it as good as Australia, though? That's the point, isn't it?" She gave an impish twisted smile.

"Is anywhere ever like home?" was all Eileen would allow herself to answer.

"You're quite right there. Home is aye where the heart is. Well, do you see yon big trees up on the hill over the bridge there. That's where the ruins are. Mind you, you'll need to cross the field so you'd maybe better have a word with the farmer first."

*　　*　　*

Tom didn't have to work so late that night, so he was home very soon after them. As usual, he related any bits of interesting happenings which he had heard or come across during the day. Then, as was also his custom, he enquired of them how they had spent their day.

"We've found our other Grannie, sure we have, Jane?"

"Another Grannie, Anna. How did you manage that?"

The childish tones rose excitedly as together they recalled the incident, detailing everything about it for his benefit.

"You know something. I think you are all enjoying living in Eaglesham. Are you?"

He had to cover his ears, so loud were their assurances that they were indeed enjoying life in the new community.

"Tell you what. It's a fine night and there's no fire lit, so what about us all having another walk. I always miss out on your best walks."

"I think they'll be too tired, Tom."

"No, Mummy, we won't be. Please, can we go?"

Eileen thought they really should be going to bed, but as she looked from their eager little faces to her husband's almost pleading one, she relented.

"Just this once, then." She laughed as she said it, for she had a feeling that this would not be the only evening walk in the summer air of Eaglesham.

The girls seemed to find a "second wind" once they were out, but Billy soon fell fast asleep in his chair.

"He's all right. The fresh air will do him good. No more disturbed nights here like we had in Cathcart, eh, Ei?"

"I'm glad of that; I was beginning to fear he'd develop bronchitis in this unkindly climate."

"It's said that Eaglesham air cures all Glasgow ills. That's why so many Glasgow folk come here on holiday."

36

"Strangely enough, someone was saying in the Post Office yesterday that the village was Glasgow's lung."

"One of them, anyway, I suppose."

"Did you ever hear that there were Covenanters buried in Eaglesham?"

His hearty laugh rang out over the moor road.

"Where's the connection?"

She had to laugh herself, then.

"None, really. I just remembered somebody else in the Post Office speaking about the Covenanters' gravestone in the churchyard."

"I see. I just wondered whether you were planning on burying me beside them, or what."

"It's more likely that you'll have to bury me some day. I would rather like to lie in a quiet little place like Eaglesham."

"What a cheery subject! Let's change it."

"Back to the Covenanters, then. Did you know there were some here?"

"I had heard that was how the Picket Law Dam was so named: because the Covenanters positioned their pickets there to give warning if an enemy approached."

"Doesn't it seem awful to think that people were persecuted and often killed for their faith?"

"Even worse to think it was their own countrymen, and sometimes kinsmen, who made them suffer."

"Wasn't it the King's soldiers from England who routed them?"

"There's a story that a company of Covenanters were being addressed by Richard Cameron at a spot known as the 'Minister's Knowe'—a secluded part in the moors when a mounted company of dragoons, led by a Sheriff from Eaglesham, ordered them to disperse in the name of the king. Cameron is supposed to have told him they owned allegiance only to the King of Kings and the Sheriff and dragoons rode off again."

They talked of scenes which would have taken place long before on the very ground they walked over that warm, pleasant evening when the two little girls ran happily ahead of them and were loathe to go indoors.

"I tell you what. We'll take your Mum down to the Churchyard and look for the Covenanters' stone with her."

"What is a Covenanter, Daddy?"

Tom went into great detail as he related to his elder daughter all the story of the brave men who refused to give up their beliefs, preferring to die at the hands of those in authority than do so.

They reached the Church gateway, a simple opening in the stone wall which enclosed the octagonal building and its surrounding graveyard, and entered its precincts with due gravity.

Eileen had never been in an old graveyard before and was quite speechless as she read first one headstone inscription and then another. They told such stories—laments almost—and were totally different to the few burial grounds she had known at home, with their simple green mounds.

She stood for a long time reading one particular inscription, her face registering her thoughts. Tom joined her to investigate the cause of her troubled expression.

"Think of that, Tom. A poor soul who lived here once lost her husband, her mother and several of her own children within a few short years."

"Times were really hard then and life brought many tragedies," was all he replied.

Jane had run on ahead and was avidly looking at the inscriptions on the different stones. She stopped eventually before a large memorial headstone in a corner and Eileen watched the intense expression on her young features as she stood solemnly reading the inscription. As they approached her, she turned away—with a thoughtful, withdrawn look in her eyes—from the martyrs' grave.

Later, as Eileen tucked her daughter into bed, she learned what lay behind the look.

"Mummy, does anybody still have to die for what they believe?"

"Not in this part of the world, anyway, my dear. Don't worry your head about that, now. Just you go to sleep." Even as she re-assured the child, she spared a thought for the brave souls who stood up to even a martyr's death for the things they so fervently believed.

Returning to the little kitchen again, she found Tom dozing in his chair. Quietly she found writing paper and pen, settled down at the scrubbed deal table and proceeded to write a letter to one of her younger sisters. She had only just finished it when Tom wakened.

"Did you enjoy your nap?"

"I wasn't really sleeping. My subconscious was working all the time and I heard your pen scratching away at paper, so I guessed you were writing to your Mum."

"To Bessie, actually."

"I'll read it over for any mistakes, if you like."

Eileen was always amused at his presumption, but she handed over the letter nonetheless. Then she rose to make the supper while he read it.

Chapter 3

REBIRTH

Though the caring for three young children occupied most of Eileen's time, she managed to fit in enough leisure to indulge in searching out more of the story of the village.

When its owner, Alexander Montgomerie—Earl of Eglinton was in Europe he saw and admired a village of unusual lay-out, possibly in Italy, and his mind turned to the Renfrewshire village which had been the very first of his family's Scottish possessions. Could it possibly be made to look something like the admired continental one? His fertile mind devised a plan.

On his return home he approached the men who occupied the little homes in the scattered hamlet which was Eaglesham. His suggestion was that a new town of Eaglesham be formed, conforming entirely to a plan and lay-out of the Earl's devising which John Ainslie his architect had been commissioned to execute.

Utilising the natural slope, the plan consisted largely of two main streets with long rows of free stone houses on each and a 15-acre common between them. The ground would be let out in tack by the Right Honourable Earl, in lots of steadings duly numbered, for a period of nine hundred years. The new owners and occupiers would be entitled to certain privileges as Tacksmen of the new Town of Eaglesham but would also be required to undertake certain responsibilities. The Tacks-

man was required to build one house at least upon each single steading within five years from the term of entry. Each tenant building a house would be entitled to cut and load away whin stone and sand from the quarries and pits belonging to the Earl. His Scheme met with some staunch opposition from the people who had qualms about embarking on the erection of completely new houses as well as the unpalatable task of demolishing their present habitations. Eventually they agreed.

In 1769 the actual rebuilding programme commenced. That very year its instigator met with sudden and violent death at the hand of a poacher on his own estate.

Slowly but certainly Eileen learned to recognise the different traits of character of some of her neighbours and also came to realise their many fine qualities.

*　　*　　*

Eileen had put her little son into one of the recess beds for an afternoon nap while she busied herself in the tiny kitchen.

As she washed through some children's garments in the black iron sink beneath the single window which overlooked the long drying green stretching far up to the wooded slope beyond, her thoughts were far away.

She had been reading one of the Waverley novels which she borrowed from a kindly acquaintance and her mind turned to its author. She had heard of the great Scots writer, Sir Walter Scott, from her mother in far-off Australia many years ago. One conversation had impressed itself indelibly on her memory and it came back vividly to her as she gazed unseeingly through the sparkling glass of the simple window pane.

"I wonder if any ink will run through the veins of one of you children?" she had mused one day as she surveyed Eileen and her sisters. They had all been sitting around the old American stove which burned cosily in the detached building situated in the enclosed area close to the homestead itself. This smaller building contained her brothers' bedroom and the laundry as well as the most important room of all—the family's own living-room, where they could enjoy themselves in their own way and where their parents seldom intruded.

On that particular occasion, so unusually quiet as each of them had been engrossed in a book, their dignified mother had interrupted her gardening to look in on them.

41

Eileen herself had been the one to question the meaning underlying her mother's remark.

"Is there any particular reason why it should, Mum?"

Then they had heard her explanation. Her grandmother had come to Australia from Sligo in the west of Ireland and she had been closely related to the American writer Mark Twain, whose real name like her own was Clemens. She had also claimed relationship to Sir Walter Scott, the Scottish romanticist. Added to that, the girls' own grand-father Deighton was the grandson of one of England's (if not the world's) very first publishers.

All their laughing speculation as to which of them would wield the weapon of the pen came flooding back to her now with crystal clarity. With equal clarity came the shattering realisation that she would possibly never see any of that happy group again in mortal form.

Purposely thrusting the gloomy prospect from her thoughts, she quickly finished her task and decided that perhaps she should give a bit more thought to the writing up of her notebook.

She went through to the front room to have a look at Billy, whom she found lying curled up on top of his sisters' old teddy bear. She carefully covered both child and toy, thinking how ironic it was that this very chubby sleeping babe had been awarded a delicate china doll, dressed in fine silk clothes, as a prize in the Baby Show on board the liner coming from Sydney.

Crossing to the front window she looked out across the green grass of the Orry where her daughters were happily playing among a group of other children. As she looked at their gay dresses, made for them the previous year by her mother, her thoughts flew across the miles to where her mother and sisters would be executing exquisite embroideries on even the most mundane of garments. And she regretted having left them and travelling so far away from them.

Returning to the kitchen, she opened the smallest drawer of the plain wooden "dresser" built on the wall facing the kitchen range. The notebook lay on top of an old cigar box, which her father had given her to pack her few important documents into. The sight of the box vividly recalled the smell of his favourite cigars; she felt her throat contract and her eyes mist over.

She lifted out the notebook and shut the drawer quickly, thinking that she would write more carefully all the story of what she had learned of Eaglesham. If she couldn't do anything else for her children, at least she would keep an account of these things and perhaps one of them, or even one of their children, would appreciate her efforts at some future date.

As she lifted the lid of one of the inkpots on the elaborate silver inkstand, which had been her grandmother's wedding gift, she thought how incongruous it looked in its present setting. The plain pen she used was more in keeping. Perhaps it was just as well her parents and grandparents were on the other side of the globe.

Before commencing to write, she re-read all that she had previously written. Then she took up her simple wooden pen, rubbed its plain broad nib on a corner of a piece of soft cloth which she kept for the purpose, and proceeded with her narrative.

With the best will in the world, she set out to improve her untidy writing, but after only one page was completed, in a careful and constrained hand, she reverted, in spite of her effort, to the more accustomed backhand scrawl. After a time, she felt her fingers stiff and her back sore, and decided that was enough for the present. She noticed that there were only a couple of blank pages left in her book, so she turned back to the page where she had resumed the story, and read what she had just written:

*　　*　　*

Robert de Mundegumbri, as Lord of the parish, must have resided in a superior dwelling to all the others in the district, but so far I have been unable to trace the site of the home occupied by this first member of the family to reside on Scottish soil.

Old records reveal that Robert (1103–78), Alan (1178–1200) his son, John (1200–20) his grandson—Third of Eagleshame and First of Innerwick—who married Helen one of three co-heiresses of Robert de Kent, with whom he obtained a third part of the lands of Innerwick in East Lothian, and Sir Alan (1220–34), his great-grandson, all continued to use the Norman form de Mundegumbri.

This latter was witness to several charters, notably with Walter, Bishop of Glasgow, between 1208 and 1232. He was succeeded by his eldest son, who appears to have been the first to use the English form of the name, Sir Robert de Montgomerie, Knight, Sixth of Eagleshame (1260–85) whose son, also Sir John de Montgomerie, became Seventh of Eagleshame (1285–1357).

Many changes had taken place in Scotland since the first of the Montgomerie family had come to settle. By the time the Scots had won their independence at Bannockburn in 1314, many Scottish people were free tenants of the land they farmed, and enjoyed a measure of prosperity. Instead of working their own territory only after their feudal lord's work was done, the husbandman was free to work his own ground all the time. Though Scottish nobles were then having strong castles built for their families, common people lived in humble fashion and had to labour for all they possessed in a continual round of work, in order to feed and clothe themselves. Everything the village needed, had to be provided by the village.

They had wood to collect and peat to cut to make fires for their homes. Sheep had to be shorn and their wool made into a coarse cloth called hodden grey, and often they cultivated flax to spin and weave into linen.

The humble dwellings had to be kept in good repair to withstand the rough weather. When they reached the state of being beyond repair, they had to be pulled down and rebuilt. They were mostly constructed of natural stone on a wooden frame, and the roof was formed with turf or heather. They left a hole in the roof, though not directly over the fire, to allow smoke to escape.

Wooden doors and shutters, as well as the simple furniture (mostly little more than table and benches) and the necessary implements, all had to be made. It took children as well as parents all their time to perform the many tasks of daily life.

Certain villages or "touns" derived their name from that of the founder, as in Symington, being simply Symon's "toun". Some of the larger hamlets or villages were created "burghs" by being given a charter, a grant of its rights, privileges and duties all duly written and sealed. If this was granted by the king, then it became a royal burgh, but if by a lord then it became a burgh of barony. If the Church, who at one time owned almost half the feudal lands, granted it, then it was likewise a burgh of barony.

People learned to trade in these burghs, which brought about a new way of living. Instead of doing all their labour for their own needs, they learned to specialise in making one kind of thing and selling it, or doing one class of service and charging for it. In this way the poorer people earned money, previously a commodity exclusive to the wealthy, and gained the freedom to buy what they wished. Skilled men from England,

Normandy and places like Flanders soon came to settle in Scotland's burghs.

Merchants lived completely by the profits made by buying from one group or class and selling at a higher price to another. Those burghs which were situated near a Castle benefited most, because they had the custom of those with most money and more expensive taste. Buying and selling were carried out on approved market days at stalls in the market place. Localities had to be granted the right to hold a market or fair and were only permitted to do so at given times.

These days, therefore, became important events in the life of the local communities of their settings, and in the surrounding hamlets and villages. Luxuries brought by merchants from abroad were on sale, as were great varieties of articles made by the burgesses, residents of the burgh. Travelling acrobats and minstrels were sometimes hired by the burghs to entertain the buyers and draw larger crowds to the stalls. Moneyed people came to purchase; poorer classes came to enjoy "all the fun of the fair" or even to simply stand and stare.

Neither progress nor prosperity had come easily; nor had independence, either for individual or nation. During the reign of Alexander III (1249–86) the Viking enemy had been defeated—in 1263 at the Battle of Largs, which signalled the end of Norse invasions of Scotland—and agreed to return the Hebrides to the Scots. Peace reigned across the border with England and it looked like a "Golden Age" until the King's death at Kinghorn changed things and ushered in unsettling times.

After the death of Alexander, the Crown passed to a girl—Margaret, "Maid of Norway"—following whose death, Scotland had no direct heir to its throne. Various contenders were ready to declare war against one another to establish their claim and Edward I of England was asked to select the successor. After asserting himself as overlord, he chose John Baliol, appointing him as his puppet King of the Scots.

When Edward made a demand on the Scots for both men and money to wage war against France, he overstepped his authority. A council of barons arranged for an Alliance with France (Auld Alliance—1295) to be drawn up against Edward. However, the latter soon subdued most of the country, as he had previously done in Wales, and stationed his nobles and soldiers strategically throughout Scotland. He even removed their records of state and Stone of Destiny, used at the crowning of their kings, to England.

The ordinary people of Scotland had no love for the English, but most of the nobles swore an oath of homage to the English king. Among a list of those who swore fealty to Edward I in 1295 is Sir John de Montgomerie, Seventh of Eagleshame.

Not many miles from his domain a knight's son was born in another Renfrewshire village, Elderslie. He lived to be a national hero, William Wallace, who led an army of the common folk against the English, driving them from the south-east of Scotland. Realising that he would not be able to keep the Scots under control until he was quit of their

leader, Edward managed to have him handed over by the trickery of one of the Scottish knights who had submitted to the English king. He was tried for treason (to a king whom neither he nor many of the Scots recognised) and condemned to death. He died for Scotland in 1305. Edward deserved his title "Hammer of the Scots", having Sir William Wallace executed at Smithfield and showing his authority by posting even more soldiers in every Scottish castle and burgh.

About the same time as King David I gave Eaglesham and other land to Walter FitzAlan, he gave Annandale to another Norman friend. One of the latter's descendants, a man of rank and property, was prepared to give up his English possessions to fight for the freedom of Scotland. His name was Robert the Bruce. He was crowned in secret in Scone, as Robert I, King of Scotland, in 1307.

During the 22-year period of his reign, in which he achieved one victory after the other against the English enemy, ultimately overthrowing them and securing the country's independence, Scotland became a free nation, their independent status being formally recognised and admitted by the English in 1328 by the Treaty of Northampton.

Alexander de Montgomerie was the next lord of the parish of Eaglesham. He was son of Sir John, who swore the oath of homage to Edward, and it is recorded that in 1358 he obtained, from England, a passport to go abroad with his retinue of sixty horse and foot. He was the Eighth of Eagleshame (1357–80) and in 1360 his son Sir John de Montgomerie married a cousin Elizabeth.

This lady was the daughter and sole heiress of Sir Hugh (or Hew) de Eglinton of Eglinton whose wife Egidea was a sister of King Robert II, first of the Stewart line and grandson of King Robert the Bruce. (He was the only son of Marjory Bruce, Robert I's eldest daughter, and Walter FitzAlan, 6th High Stewart, whose ancestor had conferred the lands of Eaglesham on the Montgomeries in the first instance, as a marriage dowry of his own daughter Marjory.) With this latest marriage, the extensive estates of Eglinton and Ardrossan (following on Sir Hugh de Eglinton's death—soon after 1376) became the property of Sir John de Montgomerie of Eglisham or Eagleshame, who quartered the arms of Eglinton with his own. Thus he was Ninth of Eagleshame and First of Eglinton and Ardrossan (1380–98).

Although the Wars of Independence were Scotland's most glorious years, welding the common people into a nation, victory had taken a heavy toll. Fighting resulted in a heavy loss of life, which caused a lack of men to tend the land properly. The scant crops proved too meagre to feed the people and famine overtook many.

Added to all this, the terrible bubonic plague which had started in China, crossed Asia to South Russia, then passed along the trade routes all over Europe (probably carried by fleas in bales of goods) had struck relentlessly in Britain also. The Black Death it was aptly named for some estimates put it that one in four of the Scottish population died.

When Robert II became king on the death of David II, Robert the Bruce's son in 1371, he had hoped for a period of peace with England, but 2,000 French knights came to Scotland to join in a raid against the English. They were not successful and in 1385 England's King Richard II inflicted a reprisal by coming north with an army and burning Edinburgh, Perth and Dundee as well as Melrose and Dryburgh Abbeys.

In 1388 the Scots retaliated. Troops under the Earl of Douglas and other men of rank, advanced into Sir Henry Percy's (Shakespeare's Harry Hotspur) land and captured his pennon. When Percy had gathered his forces, he marched "with six hundred spears, knights and squires, and eight thousand footmen—thinking that sufficient number to fight the Scots, if they were not but three hundred spears and three thousand of the others".

On a warm August night, under a full moon, a fierce battle was fought at Otterburn. The Earl of Northumberland's sons, Sir Henry and Sir Ralph Percy, were the chief sovereign captains. Many Scottish noblemen had marched with the young Earl James Douglas, among them Sir John de Montgomerie, Ninth of Eagleshame and the First Earl of Eglinton and Ardrossan, with his son Hugh. The fighting was cruel, with first the one side and then the other in the ascendency. Knights and their men, on both sides, fought valiantly with sword and dagger as well as with axe and spear, and ringing cries of "Douglas" and "Percy" pierced the night air.

It seemed as though the Scots were losing; then the strong and daring young Douglas came forth with his banner and cried "Douglas, Douglas", imparting new life into his fellow-countrymen. There was no lack of courage shown on either side, and, though the English outnumbered them three to one, the Scots fought valiantly. As the young Earl Douglas lay felled to the ground with an axe wound in his head and another through the thigh, he gave orders that his cousins—Sir John and Sir Walter Sinclair and Sir James Lindsay—raise up his banner again from the ground where it lay, and go forth crying "Douglas", but not allowing any to know that Douglas lay dying.

The battle continued fierce and cruel to the very end, when the English recoiled and yielded to the Scots. "Then the Scots were courteous and set them their ransoms and every man said to his prisoner, 'Sir, go and unarm you and take your ease: I am your master,' and so made their prisoners as good cheer as if they had been brethren, without doing them any damage".

Sir John de Montgomerie and his son Hugh captured Sir Henry Percy, a son of the Earl of Northumberland.

POLNOON STREET, EAGLESHAM.

5. Polnoon Street before the motor-car became popular

6. Foot of Polnoon Street, early 1920's

Resulting from this success in battle, a substantial edifice was erected on the eastern boundary of the parish; ransom for the release of his distinguished prisoner. This new residence for the Montgomeries was called Polnoon Castle, or "Poynded" Castle (derived from the Scots Law term—*poynd* or *poind*) and under its roof frequent guests, from the surrounding areas and further afield also, were entertained by the Earl and his successors for many long years.

It was obviously built for defence, as its few remaining fragments of walls show a thickness of eight feet. Most of its stones were eventually utilised in the building of the tweed mill which was erected nearby at Millhall. Tradition has it that a secret underground passage led from the Castle to the nearby burn, a tributary of the River Cart.

Such were the fruits of victory—but it had its price, for Sir John lost his son Hugh in the battle. The axe which was used in the famous conflict, celebrated in the old ballad "The Battle of Otterbourne", was handed down with the title through successive generations.

Each man to hold the title down the centuries had a colourful life story. In 1423 Sir John's son, also named John, who had succeeded his father in 1398, was one of the men held as hostage for the ransom of King James I, when he was held prisoner by the English.

His son and successor, Sir Alexander de Montgomerie, was much employed at court and was on several embassies to England in the reigns of both James I and James II. He was raised to the peerage as the first Lord Montgomerie. During his lifetime his king was tragically killed when one of the cannons blew up at the fight to win back Roxburgh Castle from the English.

In his great-grandson's lifetime the young Prince James, son of King James III and Margaret of Scandinavia, was captured by barons who opposed the King, setting the Prince up as their king. Lord Montgomerie attached himself to the party of the younger James. At Sauchieburn in 1488 the two Jameses, father and son, faced each other in battle. The father, King James III, was thrown from his horse and stabbed to death by an unknown hand.

The son, King James IV, raised Hugh, the third Lord Montgomerie and great-grandson of the first, to the dignity of Earl of Eglinton in 1507. His son John was killed in 1520 in "Cleanse the Causeway" (an Edinburgh fray) and the title passed in 1545, on the death of the 84-year-old Earl, to John's son Hugh who died only one year later.

Since the time when the Hotspur's capture provided the family with their castle home a mile or so from the village of Eaglesham, many exciting changes had taken place all around. In Europe there was a rebirth of learning—the Renaissance as we now call it—which was to put an end to the Middle Ages or Medieval times, and herald in a new modern age. Great sea voyages were undertaken, leading to the discovery of "The New World" of the Americas and proving the world to be round and not flat, as men had previously believed. All kinds of new things, places and people were discovered. Countries placed nearest the newly discovered lands benefited most from the trade with the new continent. Scotland was one such.

There was a darker side to Scotland's story at that time. Although her king, James IV, was the means of creating better educated Scots by ordering the barons and freeholders to send their eldest sons to be educated at grammar schools, he was also the cause by which many of the finest of Scotland's sons were slain.

In 1513 King James IV declared war on England's King Henry VIII, who was at that time fighting the French. At a fierce battle on Flodden Hill, the English proved their superiority of arms and slaughtered thousands of Scotland's best men in a dreadful and brutal massacre. James himself was killed—fighting at the forefront of his troops. His son and successor, King James V, who had married a French woman, Mary of Guise, died from a broken heart when King Henry VIII's army routed his troops at Solway Moss in 1542. He was succeeded by his infant daughter, the famous Mary, Queen of Scots.

The third Hugh, 3rd Earl of Eglinton (1546–85), had the honour of entertaining the young queen, and possibly the four Maries who attended her, while she was on a visit to Ayrshire. It is recorded that in August 1563 Queen Mary attended the Marymass Fair in Irvine, and while in the area she resided at Lord Eglinton's. It is highly probable that the royal party enjoyed good hunting in the wooded countryside.

At the ill-fated Battle of Langside, reputedly on part of the Montgomerie Lands, the Earl of Eglinton and his men engaged on the part of the Queen. For this, he was declared guilty of treason by the Regent's Parliament, but sentence was suspended. He lived until 1585, when he was succeeded by another Hugh, the 4th Earl of Eglinton.

This unfortunate man was shot dead within a year of his succession, by a Cunningham, member of a family who were ancient enemies of the Eglinton family. A kinsman, the Laird of Skelmorlie, later deeply avenged this murder.

50

Every generation of the noble family of Eglinton seems to have had at least one colourful member in its ranks. A great many mentions of Eglintons are made in all the old books of Scotland's story.

Perhaps the man who shaped the future of all who lived on his land, more than any who had gone before him, was the most praiseworthy of the whole line.

The Tenth Earl of Eglinton, who succeeded his father when only six years old in 1729, took a greater interest in the scattered dwellings which formed the hamlet of Eaglesham, than any of his predecessors had done. He was Alexander Montgomerie, Governor of Dumbarton Castle and a Lord of the Bedchamber to King George III. Village folk and gentry alike held a high opinion of this man, who did much to improve agriculture in Scotland in his lifetime.

During his travels, he took note of interesting points and often introduced what he had seen elsewhere to his own land. While in Europe, he admired a village which was vaguely similar to Eaglesham and occasioned him to consider a bold plan.

He visualised a complete new town, laid out in an orderly but attractive design, on his land in Renfrewshire where the sprawling hamlet of Eaglesham then existed.

After his return, he set about putting his idea into practice and engaged the services of a certain architect, John Ainslie, in the drawing of a plan for the new Eaglesham of his imagination.

The basic idea was that, instead of rows of houses facing each other across a main roadway, as some of the newly formed towns and older villages had, Eaglesham would have two main thoroughfares with long rows of houses on one side only. Instead of the more usual form of lay-out, with a square as focal point, it would take the form of a letter "A" and the large green or common between the two rows of houses would be intersected by another road, forming the crossbar of the "A" of the plan.

He approached the men who occupied the old, and mostly humble, homes in the tiny hamlet tucked in a gentle declivity of the corner of his extensive land, near Polnoon Castle. His suggestion that they demolish their existing homes and build new ones, to his design and within the framework of his plan, with the help of materials of his providing, met with some staunch opposition.

As well as being granted certain privileges, the residents of the new town would be required to accept specific responsibilities, and agree to build within five years. After a time, the scheme was agreed to and the rebuilding of Eaglesham commenced.

On the 24th October of the same year of 1769, Earl Alexander was out driving on his Ardrossan estate when he confronted a trespasser, who he recognised as an ex-Army officer and now Excise officer. He had previously had occasion to admonish the man, Mungo Campbell, for poaching on his land. He ordered his coachman to stop, alighted from the coach, asked the driver to wait, advanced unarmed towards Campbell and demanded the surrender of his gun. As the Earl stepped forward to take it, Campbell shot him at close range.

Although everything was done for him, the Earl—a man in his prime—died.

The rebirth of Eaglesham had begun—but the people who were to inhabit the new town suffered a great loss in the death of its originator. He was an outstanding man in very many ways and the present Eaglesham is a fitting memorial.

Chapter 4

FULFILMENT

Sunny days gave way to colder ones, as in every year, and Eileen had more time to consult both local people and written pages, in her effort to supply her growing appetite for knowledge.

Everything relevant to the locality where she now found herself, and the family who had owned it, was of great interest to her. Bit by bit, she increased her store of knowledge until she could proceed with her narrative.

The successor of the unfortunate Alexander, his brother Archibald, proceeded with the affairs of the building of the new town of Eaglesham.

Various styles and sizes of new houses began to appear within the confines of the area designated for the new town, among them one for the Earl's Factor.

The remains of the old church of the hamlet were removed and a new octagonal shaped building was erected.

Soon after the new church was built, a large mill building took shape on the common area. More houses had to be erected to supply the needs of incoming workers required to operate the mill.

A member of the Montgomerie family had married her cousin James Boswell, and was called upon to act hostess to Dr. Samuel Johnson. During his stay in Scotland the doctor was "adopted" by Susanna, Countess of Eglinton. Years later, Boswell published a book, now famous, in which he told of the visit, along with many other incidents. It was Alexander, the 10th Earl of Eglinton, who had introduced Boswell to London in his youth, and looked after his welfare.

Twenty years later a fellow countryman published another book based upon life in part of the Eglinton's land. It, too, proved immensely popular.

Eileen obtained copies of each and thrilled at the thought of living so near the setting of what she learned were famous books. Coming as she did from the world's newest continent, the sense of history all around her in Eaglesham never failed to stir her imagination and captivate her. She read avidly of life in the Castle home of the family who had owned the spot where she lived and her children played.

*   *   *

The summer was pleasant but much too short for Eileen's liking. The autumn tints and tones of the trees and hedges had been a great delight, but they had gone, too. Almost brutally, winter had descended.

The afternoon walks became a brisk half-hour tour of the village's two main streets, Montgomery Street and Polnoon Street, calling at the little stores for provisions. These were really parts of the houses; usually the main room which opened directly on to the front street, was fitted with a simple bench running at right angles to the door. On this stood various jars and bottles, with a balance or scale at the end furthest from the door. Rows of wooden shelves, on metal brackets, were fitted to the wall behind this humble counter. On them rested a wonderful selection of everyday necessities, arranged with neither rhyme nor reason, Eileen often thought.

When she returned from these walks, usually making a point of being in the vicinity of Gilmour Street just as the school children were coming out, it always gave her a warm glow to glimpse the cosy scenes of family life, through the low windows of the village homes.

On reaching the comfort of her own little place, further up the hill in Montgomery Street, she always lit the oil-burning lamp (which never ceased to remind her of the ones on the farms in far-off Orange), drew the heavy curtains, poked life into the fire in the kitchen range and made steaming hot cocoa drinks for the children and herself. While she was doing this, the girls watched the bread slowly browning on the swivel toaster attached to the side of the fire-box on the gleaming range. They always relished their hot-buttered toast with their drinks of cocoa, and as she watched the simple enjoyment on their young faces, she found ample compensation.

When they were eventually settled cosily into their beds "through the room", as she had learned to term the only other apartment of her home, she often took out the large bound book, which she had bought as a continuation to the little notebook, and proceeded with her personal history of Eaglesham and the Earls who had owned it. Sometimes Tom sat, companionably and contentedly, in his chair on the other side of the fire reading the evening paper; sometimes he had meetings to attend in Glasgow before coming home later in the evening. Either way, she found she had more time to devote to her own pursuits, which more often than not turned out to be connected to her quest for the story of Eaglesham's past.

She had been sitting in the big chair which she had come to think of as Tom's, one evening when he had been rather later than usual. On the floor beside the chair lay a bundle of socks and stockings, with a wicker workbasket beside them. When she had sat down in front of the inviting fire, she had done so with every intention of darning the assortment of hosiery.

Instead, she had sat looking into the dancing flames and allowing her mind to wander.

Deciding that the mending could wait until another time, she rose from her comfortable seat and drew an old straight-backed simple kitchen chair into position at the table. Crossing to the dresser drawer, she lifted out her handwritten book and proceeded with her story.

*   *   *

Earl Alexander, though a mature 46-year-old, had never married. Following his unexpected and tragic death, the titles and estates passed to his only surviving brother, Archibald. Thus it was really Archibald, the 11th Earl of Eglinton, who saw most of the rebuilding of the village, or more correctly the building of the new town of Eaglesham from 1769 onwards. Some old records testify that it was really he who planned it in the form of the letter "A"—which was, of course, the first letter of his name also.

In the same year of 1769 James Boswell, the son of Lord Auchinleck, a Scottish judge, married his cousin, Peggy Montgomerie of Lanislaw, whose deceased father had been related to Lord Eglinton.

The Earl actually introduced the young Boswell to London and looked after him personally while there.

Writing his *Journal of a Tour to the Hebrides*, Boswell records on the 1st November 1773, that he insisted Dr. Johnson go with him and visit the "Countess of Eglintoune, mother of the late Earl Alexander and the present Earl Archibald". Of the deceased he wrote:

"All who knew his lordship will allow that his understanding and accomplishments were of no ordinary rate. From the gay habits which he had early acquired, he spent too much of his time with men, and in pursuits far beneath such a mind as his. He afterwards became sensible of it, and turned his thoughts to objects of importance; but was cut off in the prime of his life. I cannot speak, but with emotions of the most affectionate regret, of one, in whose company many of my early days were passed, and to whose kindness I was much indebted".

Though Dr. Johnson had been lazy and averse to move, he was nonetheless delighted with the reception he received from the eighty-four-year-old Countess, Susanna, a daughter of Sir Archibald Kennedy of Culzean. Boswell has it that she was (for all her advancing years) still a very agreeable woman . . . had all the elevation . . . such birth inspires . . . figure majestic . . . manners high-bred . . . reading extensive . . . conversation elegant. She had been the admiration of the gay circles of life, and the patroness of poets.

During the course of conversation, it transpired that Lady Eglintoune was married the year before Dr. Johnson was born; this reflection caused her to remark that she might have been his mother and that she there and then would adopt him, confirming her words by embracing him as the two gentlemen took their leave, and saying, "My dear son, farewell!" Dr. Johnson had to admit to his travelling companion that he had done well to force him out.

A short time later both of them were being entertained at Sir Alexander Dick's home and Boswell trotted out the story. He blundered, however, in his chronology, stating that her ladyship adopted him as her son, in consequence of her having been married the year after the Doctor's birth. The latter pulled him up on it, pointing out that he was defaming the countess. A lady of breeding in the company saved the day with her remark, "Might not the son have justified the fault." This compliment flattered Dr. Johnson to such an extent that on subsequent discussions about his tour of Scotland, he insisted on Boswell relating it to those present.

The ex-army officer, Mungo Campbell, was tried for the murder of Earl Alexander and convicted, after a somewhat drawn-out trial. On the 28th February 1770, the morning after his trial, he hanged himself in prison. His body was about to be given for dissection but his counsel interfered and he was buried at Salisbury Crags. The Edinburgh rabble, however, dug up the body, and tossed it around until they were tired. Finally, some of Campbell's friends had the body sunk in the sea.

Some years later, a discussion about the case of Mungo Campbell arose between Dr. Johnson and a fellow guest at the home of Dr. Thomas Taylor. The English yeoman, according to Boswell, asserted "Lord Eglintoune was a damned fool to run on upon Campbell, after being warned that Campbell would shoot him if he did." The Doctor's angry retort was, "He was not a damned fool: he only thought too well of Campbell."

Meantime, at the little hollow set amid bleak, windswept moors and rocks of volcanic origin, nestling in a corner of the vast estates of the Eglinton family, men were busy. The tiny hamlet of Eaglesham, the first possession of the first generation of the Montgomeries on Scottish soil, was being transformed.

After the initial resistance to the concept of a new community had been broken, the menfolk set to work with a will. The plans which the Earl had commissioned were rigidly adhered to. The large common, between the two long rows of new building feus, was referred to in the title deeds drawn up for the various feuars, as "the area". Its trees and grass were not to be disturbed, no cattle were to be allowed on it, but the householders were to be allowed the right to use it to bleach their linen. They were also allowed the use of the water of the Lynn Burn which ran throughout the entire length of the area. Another condition of these titles granted the holders the right to cut peat for fuel from the moors above the village.

Each party who contracted to build one of the new properties, on the feus or tacks laid out according to Ainslie's plan, was furnished with a Transcript of Tack between The Commissioners of Lord Eglintoun and . . . ? whatever name the building and ground were to be registered under.

This document set out in clear terms all that was required of the new homeowners in the new town or toun. It also gave clear indication of what they were, and were not, allowed to do with their portion of land, as in the instance of growing and cutting down trees. Those growing when the land was split into lots, had to be left as they were, being "expressly Reserved as the property of the said Earl and his successors to be disposed upon by them at their pleasure".

The humble new landholders were afforded the privilege of cutting and carrying away stone from the quarries, and sand from the pits, belonging to the Earl, in sufficient quantity required for the building of their houses. They were given the space of five years from the term of their entry, to build one house at least on each single steading, and above that proportionately. There was no maximum limit stipulated, but the new homes were not to be "less than eighteen feet wide over the walls", and "no lower than eight feet with a tabling on the top of the walls".

An eight-foot-wide opening was to be left between each two steadings, or four feet at each end of the houses in the case of a double tenement, and at least eight foot high as an entry into the yards. Each tenant or tacksman was to make and maintain a road or street of not less than twenty-four feet width, and a causeway of at least six foot width, opposite his own house or tenement, at his own expense. Likewise the portion of "the area" or banks on the side of the burn, opposite their building, was to be cleared of all hedges, shrubby dykes and stones, and levelled off. For the first year, they were given the privilege of sowing, reaping and disposing of one crop of grain only upon the ground they so cleared, providing they sowed hayseed and white clover along with the grain. They were also to have the benefit of the first year's crop of hay that would be produced thereon. Thereafter, the benefit of the hay cut from the common was to be reserved for the Earl and his successors.

Arrangements were also set out for the cleanliness of the new town. No one was to be allowed to put any rubbish of any kind on the common or area, or on the street, in front of his house.

A Piper "properly cloathed with proper Bagpipes" was to be kept for the use of the inhabitants of the new town "to play thro' the Town morning and evening every lawful day" and for this musical interlude (or unmusical intrusion, perhaps, if the piper were not too good at his alloted task!) the tacksman had to fork out to the tune of one shilling sterling per steading per year. The tack (or lease) was for a 900-year period and the yearly rent and tack duty of the ground was calculated at the rate of threepence sterling for each fall (forty of which comprised a rood, or quarter-acre).

In addition, the tacksman was given "the liberty and privileges of two seats in the Kirktoun loft in the Parish Church of Eaglesham in due course with the other Tacksmen of the new Town of Eaglesham, the first subscriber for a tack or tacks in the said new Town having right to the first seats in the front of the Loft at the rate of two seats or seat-rooms for two persons for each single steading".

The ground areas differed in size, though they were nearly all the same long shape. The houses erected thereon were varied, however, being simple or elegant, small or larger, depending on the requirements and wherewithal of the intending householder.

Most of them were two-storeyed dwellings with thatched roofs. Many were only of a single storey. A few were large in comparison to their neighbours.

Facing the area, at the bottom of what is now Polnoon Street, my lord's hunting lodge, Polnoon Lodge, had been built for and used by the 9th Earl. On a cope above a door at the back of the house "W.F. 1733 A.D." was inscribed.

Directly opposite the lodge, across the area, one of the larger houses was built. It bears strong resemblance to the architecture of Polnoon Lodge. The fact that it sits well back from the line of building, as stipulated by the new village plan, might suggest that it was even a forerunner of the new planned buildings. Its first recorded possessor was a Lieutenant Matthew, thought to be a Factor to the Earl. It was known as "the Factor's".

Bit by bit the new village or town began to emerge, though in some parts the work was delayed to a certain extent by opposition to the Earl's scheme, from some of the Kirktoun's older feuars.

One or two of the larger houses showed considerably more taste than all the others. In some cases, it would appear that they were built with a view to being impressive. Into this category came a Georgian style building with more ornate frontage, perhaps, than any in the entire town. This is situated near the foot of Polnoon Street and was, in its days of origin, the home of the Earl's agent or Baron Bailie. It is even yet referred to as "the Bailie's house".

Although most of the original buildings sat neatly on the line of frontage, here and there are those which do not. One is Croft House in Montgomery Street, locally called the Provost's house, as it was the home of the Chairman of the Villagers' association, who was known as Provost. It sits well back from the line of building and has a small garden to the front, with pillared gateway, and was later the home of the Manager of the large Mill.

Some of the feuar's houses had outbuildings to the rear. Certain of them housed farm animals and had a hay loft in the upper portion.

In other outbuildings the cottage weavers had their looms, and all their necessary material and equipment. Sometimes hens were kept in the large expanses of ground to the back, and they used to wander in and out of the various buildings.

The sloping nature of the two main streets enabled the buildings to develop individual character and afforded more eye interest than a long, unbroken line of buildings of similar frontage would have done. The fact that some of the buildings were of single storey only, also helped to add interest to the scene.

Around 1788 Archibald, the 11th Earl of Eglinton, had a neat octagonal-shaped church built in a prominent position in the south-east corner of the new town or village. This was probably erected on the site of an older church, which was said to have been standing for the entire lifetime of the original hamlet, and may even have given the area an earlier name, "Ecclesiaholm"—the church in the hollow.

At one time, the communion elements used in the church were brought from Glasgow by a carrier on horseback through the village of Cathcart.

Some of the new houses bore their date of origin on their frontage. One single-storey building in South Street, now Montgomery Street, had the names of the couple who first owned it and the date of building, inscribed on a window lintel:

"James Kego and Jean Mitchell—1774"

and is still referred to as the house with the bridal lintel.

In the 1790's a 4-storey cotton mill was built in the centre of the large common. It had a water wheel measuring 45 feet in diameter, and of fifty horse-power, which was operated by water supplied from lochs on the moors above the village and the Lynn Burn in the Orry.

This mill was a great innovation. Not only did it provide employment to many of the owners of the new homes, but it also brought workers out from Glasgow. Soon more houses had to be built to accommodate these incomers, necessitating lengthening the two long main streets, North Street (now Polnoon Street) and South Street (now Montgomery Street). They were extended uphill, almost to the apex of the "A" shape of the plan.

The original residents, or "feuars", were now proud of their position in the increasingly important new community and would not allow the newcomers into their association.

Often such communities were made Burghs of Barony, but not in Eaglesham, though the Earl did have an agent. The tacksmen soon acted as though it were a Burgh of Barony; they called themselves Feuars, though in fact their long stretches of ground were not feus, but tacks. They formed a "Feuars' Association", calling its chairman Provost and the managers, Baillies.

After their initial resistance to the Earl's rebuilding scheme, they had thrown themselves wholeheartedly into the successful running of their new town, by organising developments and improvements of their own making and arising out of their pride in being such privileged house-holders. Very occasionally, the Earl had to bring to their notice that he was their laird—still.

Earl Archibald, in whose time most of the rebuilding took place, was an Equery to the Queen and Governor of Edinburgh Castle, among many other things. He died at Eglinton Castle in 1796.

* * *

Eileen decided that she had done enough writing for the time being. She had hardly finished putting away her pen and inkstand when she heard Tom's step on the stairs outside the kitchen window.

She hurried to the door to open it for him and was surprised to see he had a small parcel under one arm.

He pulled it out with his other hand and held it out to her, smiling broadly as he did so.

"Hello, El. I've brought you a wee present."

"It's not my birthday, or anything."

"Well, it doesn't have to be a special day for a man to buy his wife a gift, does it?" He laughed as he put both his strong arms round her waist, then squeezed her tightly to him.

"Oh, Tom. You don't know your own strength. You nearly made me drop my parcel before I have even opened it."

"Och! You never did like 'bear's hugs'."

She laughingly agreed.

"Give me a kiss, then, instead."

The parcel did reach the floor, with a thud, as he put his words into action.

61

"Now see what you've made me do."

"Don't worry. It won't harm it."

"It's just as well. If it had been eggs there would be an awful mess to clean up." Her rare laugh seemed to puzzle him.

"I'm remembering Jimmie's egg trick," she explained.

"Jimmie's egg trick," he repeated rather lamely.

"Yes, your brother Jimmie. Don't you remember?"

"No."

"Oh, you must, Tom. Remember he was having tea with us at Cathcart one night, when he told the girls that he would show them how to squeeze an egg without breaking it."

He thought for a moment, then she saw recollection of the occasion bring a broad grin to his round face.

"That's right. I remember now. He squeezed it too hard, or something, and it spluttered all over the wall."

"He let the egg move in his palm, and of course when he squeezed it, the shell broke. What a mess he made. Raw egg everywhere." She laughed again. "I don't think I'll ever forget the look on his face. His trick backfired all right that night."

"Wee Pud. He always was good for a laugh."

When Tom was settled down to his evening meal, which she had kept warm for him in the oven at the side of the range fire, Eileen prepared to investigate the interesting-looking parcel.

It was neatly wrapped in shiny brown paper and secured tightly with string. Although not overlarge, it was fairly heavy. It was of an irregular shape, too.

She turned it over in her hands to gain a better impression of the contents, when it dawned on her what they were.

"It's more books. You will be encouraging me to neglect my duties." She tried to sound censorious, but was so pleased at the prospect of having books to own, instead of borrow, that she knew she failed.

"I'm not afraid of that. I hope you don't mind, but they are just old books."

"Sometimes they are the better for that."

She eagerly unwrapped them and was thrilled to see that the larger volume was an early edition of Boswell's *Life of Johnson and The Tour to the Hebrides*. The second one was a stranger to her: it was entitled *Annals of the Parish* and written by a Thomas Galt.

"Oh, Tom, that's a lovely surprise." She laid them aside and, in spite

62

of his mouth being full of stewed apple and custard, gave him a resounding kiss.

"I was doing work for a man who owns a second-hand book shop in Cowcaddens a few weeks ago. I asked him if he could get me anything about Scotland in the past. When I looked him up in his shop today, he let me have these home to see if they were any use to you."

Eileen didn't like to tell him that she had already read quite a lot of the bigger book, which she had borrowed, and from which she had gleaned some information now written in her own book. Nor did she wish him spending money on her which he could ill afford. She hesitated, causing him to study her expression.

"Do you not think they'll be any use?"

"I don't want you spending money to indulge my whims."

"The fellow said if you would like them, they were mine for five bob. I think I can rise to that all right."

As he seemed to have struck a good bargain, and so as not to disappoint him in his unusual role of beneficiary, she refrained from mentioning that she had already perused one—and never heard of the other.

"They will be very helpful in my hobby. Thank you," was all she responded.

"Seemingly the Galt's one is about Irvine in Ayrshire more than a hundred years ago."

"That's where the Eglintons lived." Eileen was immediately curious to find out whether there was any mention of the family in it. She glanced quickly through its pages and found that the writer did refer to its members.

"Is it? Who are they?"

"Do you mean to say you haven't heard of the great family of Eglinton who owned all the land about here?" She really did not think he could have failed to hear of them, sometime or other.

"Can't say I have. I always thought this place was supposed to have been owned by a Duke. Wait a minute, though, isn't that the name of the people you were writing about in a letter to Bessie?"

"Of course it is. And in my notebooks, too."

He grinned impishly over to her.

"You're tormenting me, Tom. You knew all the time. In fact, you probably even asked the bookseller man if he had anything about the old family."

He laughed at the dawning awareness of his actions as it registered on her face.

"That's right, my dear. How did you guess? Now you can read about all the people who lived hereabouts when your country only knew the aborigines."

She reflected in silence on his statement.

Tom finished his meal and started to clear away. She knew he was doing so, but didn't rise to help with the washing-up as usual. Her thoughts were years away.

"Is there anything the matter?" Tom's voice sounded a little bit apprehensive, and that succeeded in rousing her from her reverie.

She jumped to her feet and crossed over to the sink.

"No, nothing at all. I was just thinking how strange it is that our children actually play about on the very spot where lords and ladies used to ride years ago."

He looked closely at her.

"The whole of society is changing these days, so is there anything so strange about that?"

"There certainly is, to my mind."

7. Gilmour Street at the Cross, the early 1920's

8. Eaglesham House

Chapter 5

DOOM

The "Festive Season" arrived and Eileen found herself comparing it with past Christmases celebrated thousands of miles away.

During the cold winter months she had made the acquaintance of an old lady nearing her ninetieth birthday, a native of the village who remembered Eaglesham when it was at the peak of its prosperity. She told of her life and the things she remembered most, enthralling both Eileen and her little daughters with her style of reminiscing.

On one occasion, she told them about a cousin who had been "in service" in Eglinton Castle and had given all the members of her wide family circle a first-hand account of the grand tournament held in its park, and of the deluging rain which washed it out.

Eileen obtained a book which confirmed everything the old lady said and read in it that the 13th Earl who had organised it, was possibly influenced to a large extent by the writings of Scotland's own romanticist, Sir Walter Scott. In her own childhood in Australia, Eileen had heard her mother speak of a family connection to Scott.

As a result of the financial losses sustained by the Earl on account of the catastrophic tournament, which had been attended by almost 100,000 people, the parish and new town of Eaglesham had to be sold to offset the debts incurred. In 1844 Allan Gilmour, timber importer, became the new owner of the estate of Eaglesham.

From about that time onwards, the village's prosperity began to decline and its population started to diminish again. A major blow befell it when its large mill was burned down in 1876, resulting in the workers leaving the village and going elsewhere for employment. By the turn of the century, the population had almost halved.

During the first decades of the twentieth century, many of the little houses were occupied by elderly, often poor, people. Some of them watched the Australian woman with her two young daughters and baby son; they took note, too, of her husband.

Early in the new year, Tom managed to find unfurnished accommodation in Cathcart Road, Crosshill, which would be nearer his place of employment.

*   *   *

Winter weather continued and the Australian in Eileen's make-up rebelled against its chilling ways. Christmas was only a few days off and her thoughts were often with her parents, and the various members of her family, on the other side of the world.

She recalled the wonderful times they had been used to on Christmas Days when they were all young. Like her own mother and father, most of the couples in the family circle had large families. Christmas was the time when they all came together in the old house, which was her great-grandmother's home: her great-grandfather, Joseph Moulder, had died twenty years or so before her own birth.

What Christmas parties they had there! Endsleigh House was set in its own private park of more than five hundred acres, quite large even by Australia's vast land standards. The farm stretched to the back and one side of the estate. Near the house was an enclosed garden, set within a very large and lovely garden of brilliantly flowering native shrubs and bushes. In front of the house, their branches affording welcome shade, was quite a large orchard. Here all the children, of the various branches of the Moulder family, had their Christmas dinner picnic style while their elders had theirs in more dignified fashion indoors, coming on to the wide verandah at times with their glasses in hand. Her own grandparents, Grandma and Grandpa Deighton, were always there, with her great-aunts and uncles, the Lanes, the McLachlans from Wollaroi, and others—with their families and their grandchildren. It was a great occasion for all the relatives but it was the children who looked forward to it most of all. On reflection, she thought that her kith and kin must have comprised quite a large proportion of the population of Orange in her childhood years.

She thought, then, of the preparations she had made for her own children's Christmas in Eaglesham; how meagre and beggarly they appeared by comparison. She had shopped for their presents in Glasgow while Tom took the children to see "Santa" in his lanternland in Bow's Emporium in the High Street, where they had been given "lucky dips" by the bearded, red-cloaked wizard.

Her money had been limited, so she had tried to obtain the best value possible in everything she purchased. She would dearly have loved to buy the girls a doll's pram and saw a beauty; she was shocked to read 55s. 6d. on the price tag. Instead she had looked for something carrying a more realistic price ticket, settling at last for a 7s. 6d. dressed doll for Jane and a miniature tea-set for Anna which she was assured was china, but at 3s. 11d. she felt certain it must be Delph. As Billy was too young to understand what it was all about, she limited her outlay on his present to half-a-crown—for a floating rubber frog to play with in his bath. Tom had given her money to buy whatever she wished for her own gift, but she had spent half on something for himself.

She considered that he had been very generous in giving her 30s. to spend on herself, but she had only spent 7s. 11d. of it for a rather nice pair of suede gloves. She had never worn suede in Australia, where the gloves were mostly white cotton.

Tom was sorely in need of new pyjamas, especially as those he had were thin cotton ones bought for a warmer climate, so she bought him a pair of warmer ones, in a blue stripe design. Then with what was left of the 30s. she bought a warm wool scarf, thinking it would be service-able for any one of them on an extra-cold day.

Only after she had made her purchases, when her purse was empty, did she allow herself the luxury of gazing on the lovely novelties and gifts displayed in the better stores of Glasgow's shopping centre. Beautiful tea cosies with porcelain figures, and wastepaper baskets decorated with china ladies, were among attractive Parisian goods which she fondly admired. They were pounds, though, and she only had shillings.

As she busied herself in the tiny kitchen of her house she administered herself a severe scolding. What right had she to wish for more! She had a faithful and loving husband as well as three lovely children. They had never been in real need in their lives and Tom had steady employment, even although none of his father's wonderful promises of taking him into partnership had materialised. Only the other week or so she had read in the newspaper of the "lucky few" who had been given employment by the extension of the tramways, necessitating the widening of the road from Maryhill to Canniesburn.

She could well imagine how difficult life must be for the "unlucky many" whose breadwinner was among the vast number of the un-employed, on the "buroo" as they termed it in Glasgow. She thought, too, of the many good folks even in Eaglesham whom she knew were finding it hard to make ends meet, with only casual earnings to supple-ment their small "parish relief". Scotland—or was it Britain?—was not an ideal place to live in the year 1922.

Her thoughts were in danger of making her unhappy, so she finished what she was doing, then picked up the morning paper and sat down before the brightly burning fire. She read the caption for the picture on the front page, "Young poets of England" representatives, presenting flowers and a book to Madame Tetrazzini. What peculiar names they had, she thought. Aldous Huxley, Edith, Osbert and Sachervell Sitwell. Then she thought of her own literary attempts, which she had not added to for some time.

Putting away the newspaper, she crossed to the drawer in the old dresser and lifted out inkstand and book. She re-read the last page of her own scrawling handwriting, to refresh her memory, then took up the story from where she had left off.

* * *

When Archibald, 11th Earl of Eglinton, died in 1796 he left no son to inherit his title and possessions. His first wife died when she was only 21 years old and his second wife, Frances, had two daughters. The elder one, Lady Mary Montgomerie, fell heir to most of her father's possessions.

The title passed to the son of Alexander Montgomerie of Coilsfield and Lillias, who was the elder daughter of Sir Robert Montgomerie of Skelmorlie, and succeeded her father in 1735. (This branch of the House of Eglinton was descended from George, the second son of Alexander, the first Lord Montgomerie.) He was Hugh, 12th Earl of Eglinton, whose elder son Archibald, Lord Montgomerie, dutifully married his cousin Lady Mary, the 11th Earl's wealthy heiress.

This Hugh, 12th Earl, born *c.* 1740, served during the seven years' war in America. His long military career commenced when he was only fifteen years old. When hostilities with France broke out in 1778, he was appointed major in the Argyll or Western Fencibles. In 1780 he successfully stood for Parliament and was returned in 1784. He vacated his seat, however, in 1789 on taking up the appointment of Inspector of military roads in the Highlands of Scotland.

Robert Burns wrote of him as "soldier Hugh", apparently a poor public speaker, in his work "Earnest Cry and Prayer to the Scotch Representatives in the House of Commons":

> Thee, Sodger Hugh, my watchman stented,
> If bardies e'er are represented;
> I ken if that your sword were wanted,
> Ye'd lend your hand:
> But when there's ought to say anent it,
> Ye're at a stand.

In 1793 he raised the West Lowland Regiment, of which he was the Colonel, then soon afterwards he raised the Glasgow Regiment. He was Lieutenant-General of Edinburgh Castle. In 1796 he succeeded to the titles of Eglinton, as stated, on the death of Archibald, his cousin, shortly after he was again returned to Parliament. In the same year, Nathaniel Gow published some of his musical compositions, for "Sodger Hugh" was not only an enthusiastic fiddler, but a composer. The tune "Lady Montgomerie's Reel", which is sometimes set to the Scottish Country Dance entitled "The Montgomeries' Rant" which was recorded as far back as the time of the Tenth Earl, and "Ayrshire Lasses" are probably the best known.

He was also Lord Lieutenant of the County of Ayr and Knight of the Thistle. He was created Baron Ardrossan *c.* 1806. In 1817 he succeeded to the estate of Portreehill, on the death of his sister-in-law, the Dowager Lady Cathcart of Carlton. He married his cousin Eleanor, the 4th daughter of Robert Hamilton of Portreehill.

His was a most eventful life. As well as rebuilding Eglinton Castle near Irvine, the family seat of the House of Eglinton, he initiated many and varied improvements in his estates, both in the agricultural and commercial aspects.

Great changes had taken place all around during his long lifetime. His country had at last stopped warring with their neighbours across the "border", and were learning to enjoy a new enlightenment. He was too young, when Prince Charles Edward returned to claim the throne, to have been caught up in the convulsion caused thereby, and could possibly have been more involved in the cultural revolution then taking place in Scotland's country houses, than in the Jacobite cause.

Certainly Susannah, the Dowager Countess of Eglinton (who was the third wife of the 9th Earl and mother of both the 10th and 11th Earls) was a patron of the arts, and of the early Edinburgh dance Assembly, as were her beautiful daughters.

James Watt, and others like him, had transformed the way of life for many of his countrymen. This clever man, born not many miles from Eglinton Castle, experimented with the apparatus used in the lectures given in the University of Glasgow's Natural Philosophy (science) classes. He studied different models and experimented with steam in his workshop, off King Street in Glasgow, until he mastered the principles of using steam to drive engines. He left on record how the idea occurred to him:

"It was in the Green of Glasgow. I had gone to take a walk on a fine Sunday Afternoon. I had entered the Green by the gate at the foot of Charlotte Street—had passed the old washing house, I was thinking upon the engine at the time, and had gone as far as the herd's house, when the idea came into my mind that as steam was an elastic body it could rush into a vacuum, and if a communication was made between the cylinder and another vessel, it would rush into it, and then might be condensed without cooling the cylinder. . . . I had not walked further than the golf house when the whole thing was arranged in my mind."

The cotton spinning trade was becoming established in Scotland as elsewhere in Britain, and the prospects of Watt's discovery, and developments subsequent upon it, opened up whole areas of imaginative projects. Water would soon become a thing of the past, so far as providing power for the mills was concerned.

Gas-lighting had been invented, and was used in the mills to provide longer working hours, so increasing the establishment's output. It also enabled two "shifts" of workers to be given employment. This was not to be ignored, as the first half of the eighteenth century proved.

These years, which came to be known as "The Hungry Years", held little cheer for Scotland. The poorer classes often knew hunger and misery, with the dark shadow of death never far from any home. Bad seasons following each other in quick succession, coupled with poor conditions of cultivation, were the prime factors. It was fortunate that there existed a well-established parochial system of education, which by its capable administration produced such scholars as won it the admiration and envy of larger countries. These pupils, often called "lads-o'-pairts", were sometimes sent to a University by an interested party, perhaps their local parish or land-lord. For the less ably endowed, life was mostly a hard fight for survival.

Things began to look more hopeful with the coming of machinery which would take much grind from the poor human machines, but some visionless men misinterpreted the signs of progress and could only hurl boulders at the new mechanism or set fire to the mills which housed them.

*   *   *

Noticing the time on the face of the shoddy alarm clock which sat on the "mantelpiece", Eileen realised that she had spent far too long digging into the past. It was more to the point to look to the present. If she allowed young Billy to sleep any longer, she would have trouble in putting him to bed later.

Anna was playing contentedly with some of her large family of dolls beside the fire. She sat on the only piece of carpeting which the little house boasted. Her dolls were no more than large wooden clothes pegs on the tops of which Eileen had drawn eyes, nose and mouth with crayons, and dressed them in pieces of gaily coloured cotton. One or two, dressed for a party, wore clothes of satin or velvet ribbon. The fair-haired child could hardly have looked happier had she been in a lavishly-equipped nursery tended by a private nursemaid, Eileen felt sure.

"I'm going to waken your wee brother, Anna. Are you coming through with me?"

"You should say 'Cm'on thru' the hoose', Mummy."

"Indeed I should not. That's not the proper way to speak."

"That's how all the other girls talk, then."

"Perhaps it is, dear. But I don't want you to speak like that. Do you hear your Daddy or I talking that way?"

"No, you don't. But everyone says you don't belong here, so I s'pose that's why."

71

Eileen felt that the less she made of the subject, the better, so let it rest there.

*   *   *

Jane had been told to meet them at the Cross after she came from school and was ready waiting as Eileen took Anna by one hand and pushed the baby in his chair with the other. Seeing them coming down Montgomery Street, Jane ran up past the Church and Dalgleish's shop to join them.

Eileen could tell by her face that she was excited.

"Well, what have you been up to?"

"Nothing. I'm just straight from school."

Eileen smiled. Whatever difference that fact made she couldn't tell.

"Mummy."

"Yes." Here it came. Jane never kept her guessing for very long.

"Mummy. Can I go up to the dam with the girls in my class?"

"Whatever are they going up there for in this weather?" The very thought made Eileen shiver. The dam was high up in the moors and it would be even colder there than it was in the village.

"Meg says it's great there. All the men play on the ice with stones and brushes."

Anna looked at her sister with huge eyes, then raised them to Eileen's as though seeking an explanation for Jane's queer statement.

"That must be what they call 'curling', Jane. Yes, I suppose that a lot of them will play it there."

"Can I go up and watch them?"

"No, dear. We're going to visit an old lady."

"Are we going to see our Grannie, again?" Anna piped up.

"I told you we haven't got a Grannie, didn't I." Jane helped her disclaimer home with a poke at Anna's ribs.

"Old Grannie, then. She said she was everybody's Grannie, so there."

Eileen did not like to hear her daughters squabbling in the style which threatened, so quickly set their minds at rest.

"No. We are not going to see the old lady with the puppies, if that is what you mean."

"Oh. . . . Why not, Mummy?"

72

"That is too far to walk in this cold weather. We'll go there again when it is warmer. We're going to see a different old lady this time."

Jane did not look at all pleased. "There must be an awful lot of old ladies in this place," she grumbled.

"There are," was all her mother answered.

They cut across the "Orry" by the mid road and stopped for a short time in Polnoon Street to speak to a group of Jane's school chums, not in any hurry to reach their homes. They didn't seem to be unduly worried by the cold weather, Eileen noted.

A little further up the street, they turned into a wide opening between two buildings.

"Where are we going?"

"To the old lady's house, as I said."

"Does she live up a back stair, too?"

Eileen could not help wondering what her own mother would think of her present living quarters. She dispelled the thought from her mind as quickly as she could.

"No. Just along here; the green door is hers."

"Is this a street, Mummy?"

"Not a real street, Anna. People just call it 'The Clachan'."

"Is this 'The Clachan'? A girl in my class told me an old witch lived here. Does she still?" Jane had not overcome her dislike of old women, Eileen noticed.

"Of course not. There are no such things as witches. They were all drowned long ago."

"Thank goodness for that," Jane muttered with deep conviction.

"Anyway, there would not be any living in The Clackan, I'm sure."

"Are you? It's not Clacken, Mummy, it's Clachan."

"That's right, Jane. Clacken."

"Awch! You can't talk Scotch."

"I notice you can."

They had reached the green door and Anna wanted to know if she might rap the shiny brass knocker.

"Yes, you knock it," she told her and was surprised at the alacrity with which the door was opened.

"Come awa' in. I heard the weans talkin' so I thought it would be yoursel'."

There was a huge log fire blazing in the shining grate, throwing a lovely warm glow over everything in the tidy kitchen, where a table was laid with a crisp white linen cloth and blue and white crockery.

"I'll tak' yer coat, Mistress Wallace, and ye can mak' yersel' cosy by the range. The lassies can cm'on thru' the hoose for there's a good fire here, wi' a big guard fixed."

Eileen could see that neither of her "lassies" had the slightest inclination to do so.

"On you go, girls, and play quietly."

Still they hung back, Jane even looking as though she had indeed confronted the witch she had been told about.

"Ay. There's plenty things to play wi'. I've laid them all on the mat by the fire. Tartan dollies and colourin' books and crayons."

After a little more coaxing from their hostess, the girls reluctantly allowed themselves to be led "thru' the hoose". The appeal of dolls and books must have been great as there was no further bother.

At the old lady's suggestion, Eileen laid Billy down on the woollen rug at her feet and let him kick away to his heart's content.

In the course of conversation she mentioned to her friendly hostess that she was gathering all the information which she could lay her hands on, of Eaglesham and its owners. She was delighted to learn that the old lady had stayed in it for the best part of eighty years, remembering well when the "toun" was at the very height of its prosperity.

Story after story she related to her, making them all come to life, so vivid was her portrayal. At one point, Eileen could see two excited little faces peering through from the open doorway between the two small apartments.

Seemingly, she had a cousin who was in service at the Great Eglinton Castle in Ayrshire. Many were the tales which came from there. Perhaps the most vivid of all was the story of a wonderful tournament which "His Worship, the Earl" had held in the Castle grounds. Unfortunately, the lavish preparations had been largely spoiled by prolonged heavy rainfalls.

Such was her power of narration that Eileen was surprised when she looked at the time on the carved wooden clock sitting on the top of the chest of drawers, beside the recess bed with its frilled curtains and valances.

She apologised for overstaying her welcome but was assured she had done no such thing, and bidden to come back again soon.

*   *   *

It was several weeks later that a book relating the full story of the Eglinton Tournament come into Eileen's possession for a short period. In it, she read that Sir Walter Scott had fired the imagination of his fellow-countrymen by the contents of his novels, and that the pageantry enacted on King George IV's visit to Edinburgh in 1822, the first visit of a reigning monarch for 171 years, also largely of Scott's making, might have suggested the idea of the Tournament to Earl Eglinton.

She read that Scott's novels influenced a large section of society and caused a revival of interest in medieval costumes and customs. The lavish displays put on for King George IV's visit sparked off other events and set the pattern for further costume extravaganzas, on both sides of the border. Perhaps the most remarkable of these, though, was the great baronial tournament organised by the 13th Earl of Eglinton in the grounds of Eglinton Castle on 28th August 1839, when medieval costumes and armour were fabricated for it. Ceremonies were organised and history recreated in a way which would surely have delighted Scott, who had died only about seven years previously.

She remembered her own mother telling her that Grannie Moulder, who had given them the Christmas Day parties in the orchard in Orange, was connected to Walter Scott, the Scottish writer. She read of the exciting events at Eglinton Castle even more avidly, feeling that there was something of a link with one of her own flesh and blood— although it was so slight as to be almost non-existent.

The stories she read were so gripping as to make her almost forget that she was writing something of a story herself. Almost, but not quite. One night when Tom was attending one of his meetings, she took out her well-thumbed book and brought it up to date.

*   *   *

Archibald, Lord Montgomerie, was an A.D.C. to the Duke of Wellington. He was posted to the Court of the King of Naples at Palermo, where his wife, the wealthy Lady Mary, accompanied him. They had two sons, the first born was Hugh, b. 1811 at Coilsfield and afterwards resided at Eglinton Castle. The second was Archibald William, b. in Sicily in 1812. In 1814 Lady Mary's husband died and she returned with her two infant sons. In 1817 the 12th Earl of Eglinton died and was succeeded in the greater proportion of his estates and property by his eldest daughter, Lady Mary. The titles of the greater parts of the estates, therefore, devolved upon her son, Hugh Montgomerie of Coilsfield. Soon afterwards he died of croup, at the age of only seven years. Therefore, Archibald William, the younger of the two sons, became the 13th Earl of Eglinton and subsequently Viceroy of Ireland.

When Lady Mary returned with her infant sons from Palermo, she brought some baby clothes which were made for her by a French-woman. These she lent to Mrs. Jamieson, the wife of a cotton merchant in Ayr, who used them as models for a cottage industry newly developed in Ayrshire—a very specialised form of fine needlework, mostly executed by the womenfolk in their own homes during the early 1800's. It was known locally as "The Floo'erin'" due to the fact that most of the embroidery designs used were of flowers.

Another industry which was very popular was the making of lace, which was mostly made in neighbouring Darvel. It was not unusual to see lace-makers from there, making their way over the moors and through Eaglesham, with their wares strapped on their backs, setting out to Glasgow where they sold the goods.

Perhaps one of the oldest houses of Eaglesham still standing is a tiny little building, facing the toll house, which was originally two separate weaver's cottages. The main house in front of it was probably built around 1760, but possibly the little ones were built as far back as 1690. It was between the years of 1792 and 1876 that the cotton industry reached its peak in Scotland.

In August of the year 1839 the young Archibald William, Lady Mary's younger son and 13th Earl of Eglinton, organised a most ambitious and costly Victorian Gothic extravaganza.

Reviving the favourite occupation of medieval knights and nobility, he staged a full-scale tournament, with all the elaborate preparations and lavish trappings which had always attended these events in the past.

Invitations to attend and compete in the grand tournament were sent out to a great many titled and important people throughout the country. Samuel Pratt, the London dealer, was commissioned to erect stands and pavilions in the grounds of Eglinton Castle, near Irvine. He was also required to make up suits of armour for wear by the various knights taking part in the tournament, as well as being ordered to supply large numbers of costumes for the many guests.

Preparations for the forthcoming event entailed a huge volume of work for everyone connected with the young Earl of Eglinton. Great excitement filled the air as different members of the nobility began to arrive in Ayrshire and head towards Eglinton Castle. Some were near neighbours, like James Ogilvy Fairlie of Coodham, an estate and mansion house not far from Kilmarnock, who as Knight of the Golden Lion gained the highest score on the final day of the Tournament.

Others were simply the cream of contemporary society, obvious choices for such an occasion, like Viscount Glenlyon, the Knight of the Gael, who was later attended by seventy uniformed Atholl Highlanders before the end of the lavish entertainment. Also invited were some who attended Eton at the same time as the young Lord of the Tournament.

Unfortunately, torrential rain fell for a prolonged period during the first afternoon, soaking many intricately-wrought costumes, in tartan as well as plain materials. The armour, some of it dating from the days of King Richard II, some having been specially purchased from Continental countries such as Spain and Italy, which started off burnished and gleaming, began to lose its lustre. The large marquee, which had been specially erected in the grounds for the ball to be held for the two thousand guests, had its roof badly damaged by the downpour.

Despite the weather conditions, the tournament proceeded. As near as possible, medieval customs and rituals were observed, with the various knights who took part being accompanied by Esquires and Retainers carrying weapons and wearing armour and costumes appropriate to their station. The fine Grecian-style grandstand had a special canopy for Lady Seymour, the Queen of Beauty, who was attended by Prince Louis Napoleon.

At the end of the Tournament, Lord Eglinton, Lord of the Tournament, was awarded the victor's crown. On the last day of the month, and of the whole enormous proceedings, a great medieval banquet was held in the Castle itself with all its attendant ceremony and lavish provision.

The damaged marquee had been speedily repaired by a band of workmen feverishly labouring to make good the harm caused to its roof by the heavy rain. The scene at the ball there, which was a fitting wind-up to the entire venture, was both colourful and picturesque. Male dancers provided colour in their elaborate costumes of crimson, blue and green damask and plush, decorated and trimmed with gilt and silver braid. The ladies' gowns were each a picture in themselves. Some had wide, hooped skirts, others had rich ermine trimming and a great many had long wide sleeves and draped sashes. Certain ladies wore period headdress and others carried ornate fans.

Altogether, the huge company of dancers and onlookers alike thoroughly enjoyed themselves in the vast, decorated canvas hall with its many ornamental candelabra suspended above their heads.

When all the trumpet blowing and rolling of drums had ended, and all that remained of the extravagant entertainment was a muddy quagmire in the Castle grounds, the day of reckoning fell. So great had been the drain on the family finances that it became imperative to sell property to meet the colossal debts incurred by the Tournament.

* * *

The choice was Eaglesham—the very first portion of Scottish soil to come into the family, by Robert de Mundegumbri, their Norman Knight forefather.

By the year 1844 "the whole lands and estate of Eaglesham, including the patronage of the Parish Kirk" had passed into the hands of a new owner, Mr. Allan Gilmour, founder and partner in the city firm of Pollok, Gilmour & Co. which had been established early in the nineteenth century by Mr. Allan Gilmour and Messrs. John and Arthur Pollok. The figure quoted for the sale of that portion of the Barony of Eaglesham was £200,000. On purchase of the Estate, the Gilmours occupied Polnoon Lodge for a time until their new mansion home, Eaglesham House, was built at Riverside in 1859.

At that time the making of new railways had brought many workers over from Ireland. Many lived in a tall tenement in Montgomerie Street, thus its "Paddy's Castle" nickname.

Although the railway had come as far out from Glasgow as Clarkston, the Gilmours would not allow it on their land, so the line was in the direction of East Kilbride, via the neighbouring village of Busby. This meant that potential new industry was lost to Eaglesham, for want of good transport links.

Links there were, however, in the form of a horse-drawn bus which plied between the village and the railway station at Clarkston, as well as the "Soor Milk Cairt", the farm cart which took the milk to Cathcart, as well as the odd traveller.

The new owners of the proud little new town took up residence in what had been the Earl's shooting lodge, Polnoon Lodge, and put plans in hand to have an imposing baronial-type mansion built in its own park not far from Eaglesham itself.

Little by little, changes took place in the village. Almost imperceptibly at first, the population began to decline and then a calamity struck.

The largest of the mills, the cotton spinning one in the centre of the "Orry", had for years been the biggest employer of local labour. It had always been a well-run establishment, escaping much of the trouble experienced by its counterparts in Glasgow and other industrial centres. In 1876 it was burned, badly.

The cotton industry in Scotland had reached its peak before then, and iron and steel were the interests of most business minds. Accordingly, it was decided that the mill would not be rebuilt. Not surprisingly, the millworkers, who had only come to live in Eaglesham because it afforded them employment, left the area. When the twentieth century dawned, the population of the thriving rural village had almost halved.

Up and down the two main streets, as well as through the back pends and entries, houses lay empty and forlorn. Many of the ones still occupied at that time were inhabited by elderly people, of whom a good many had never lived anywhere else. Times were hard, and Eaglesham was no different to any other place in Scotland—it had many poor families, struggling to eke out their meagre means.

Workers who had enjoyed their spell of life in the country, started to re-visit the scene of their enjoyment and soon the houses were again filled with people coming to Eaglesham from Glasgow for holidays. As in coast towns, local householders "let out" parts of their homes. Those fortunate enough to have a tiny cottage or hut at the foot of their long plots of ground, took up residence there and "let" their entire house.

*   *   *

Christmas had come and gone, bringing happy and sad moments alike to Eileen. She had been happy to see the way the children all enjoyed themselves in their unsophisticated way. Jane and Anna loved every minute, not seeming to think amiss of their own very poor presents, no poorer than many of those received by their playmates. Some of them did not have any, as their parents didn't hold with Christmas.

This seemed very strange to Eileen, who had always thought of the people of Scotland as being among the most religious of all nationalities. She had questioned Tom about it one evening, but all he could say was that it savoured too much of "paganism" for the Calvinistic streak in them, and he felt much the same himself. Thinking it best to let the matter rest there, she had said no more.

It struck her as more than simply strange, though, to see the fuss they all made about the coming in of another year—"Ne'erday" being the biggest event on their calendar, it would seem. The village publicans certainly did brisk trade and those who seldom had enough money for more than the barest of necessities, somehow found enough to buy themselves "a bottle".

She had experienced sad hours throughout the period of festivities. It was the first Christmas she had spent away from her own flesh and blood, and on the other side of the world to her beloved homeland.

Mother, father, brothers and sisters all seemed worlds away—and her heart yearned after them. Would she ever see them again, she asked herself time after time. Why had she ever agreed with Tom to come to this country anyway, when there had been no good reason to leave all they had built up together in Sydney. And certainly no good reason to come here, where they were not even wanted. Bitterness crept into her spirit at times.

In just such a mood, she tip-toed through to the front room one bitterly cold evening, leaving Tom dozing in his chair before the big fire of coal and logs burning in the kitchen range.

The unshed tears smarted behind her eyes and her throat had almost closed with the huge lump which seemed bent on choking her. The dumpy base of the oil lamp, which sat on the lid of the wooden coal bunker in the tiny "lobby", served as a further reminder of her life in sunny Australia. They had always had a little one very similar to it sitting on a side table in the big farm kitchen.

She looked at the childish faces of her three children, all sound asleep in their beds in the wall recesses. How serene they all appeared, she thought. Then her heart filled with unspoken gratitude for happy, healthy children and the fact that Tom always brought his entire wages home for the good of them all. She had learned, both at home and since leaving it, that this was far from always being the case with the heads of families.

Feeling somewhat better about things, she crept over to the chest in the corner and lifted the saucer with a burning candle on it. She crossed

9. Eglinton Tournament, Lithographs by Edward Carbould, London 1800

10.   Montgomery Street before the moor road was improved

to the single casement window and pulled aside the curtain a little. Then she caught her breath in sheer delight.

There had been a heavy fall of snow, quite unknown to her. The moon was full and shed silvery floodlighting on a scene of utter beauty. Every tree within sight was laden with pure white pillows of snow and the road and grass alike were transformed into brilliant white carpets.

She gently blew out the candle she held and opened the curtains to their full extent, allowing her eyes to feast on the scene. The houses across the "Orry" in Polnoon Street looked different. Their walls almost sparkled in the moonlight and the roofs looked as though they had been covered with huge sheets of cotton wool. The windows which had not been shuttered or had their curtains closed, looked so cosy with the glow of the lamps and fires showing warmly against the stark whiteness of the landscape. It was so much more wonderful than she had ever imagined it could be.

She had not heard Tom enter the room.

"What's wrong, Ei?"

His voice was a low whisper, so as not to disturb any of the sleeping children, but it made her start even so.

"Nothing," was all she could manage in answer.

"You'll get cold standing at the window like that. Come on back through to the fire."

The kindness of his tone, together with the pent-up emotions she had been struggling with, broke down her control.

"Come over here, Tom," she whispered on a sob.

He stood beside her at the window and she laid her head against his chest, just below his shoulder.

Without a sound, he slipped his arms around her and gave her a gentle squeeze.

"It's been snowing."

"Oh, Tom, isn't it lovely?"

He didn't answer for a long time and Eileen wondered what he was thinking. Perhaps he was worried in case he would not be able to work; she supposed that slaters would be "paid off" when it was snowing and she knew how he dreaded that happening. She certainly was not prepared for the reply she received.

"Snow is like prayer, Ei."

She thought hard for a second or two, but was unable to follow him.

"It changes things."

F

Suddenly the tears spilled over. She felt rebuked for her bitter thoughts of a few minutes before, and with a gentle tug on his hand, she allowed herself the relief of shed tears.

When they were settled in front of the fire again, sharing the last pot of tea for the day, Tom asked her what she really felt about living in their temporary home.

Thinking of all the thoughts which had so recently filled her mind, and the chastening effect of the snow, she found it impossible to make any complaints. Tom seemed both puzzled and worried, she noticed.

"Is there something wrong?"

Had there been further trouble between him and his brothers, she wondered. Or, even worse, between him and his father, on whom they were almost dependent.

"Nothing wrong, I wouldn't think. I thought you would prefer to have a place of your own, that's all."

"Of course I would. Surely you realise that, but I'll be content to stay here until you can find somewhere. Unless we have to go?" Fear caught at her imagination, then, as she fought against the thought of having to change "digs" yet again.

"We will have to go fairly soon, Ei." Then he was unable to carry on the suspense any longer. "I've got a house for you."

She thought he was tormenting at first, then slowly she realised that he was in earnest.

"Do you really mean we have a place of our own, to furnish and decorate as we like?" It seemed almost impossible.

"That's exactly what I mean. It'll take some time, of course, before we can move in. There are a few things needing doing. Jimmie and Dave have offered to lend me a hand, and I expect Bob and Hugh will, too, but they're working at Paisley, so I haven't seen them today."

"Your brothers will help you, then?"

"Of course. Didn't you think they would?"

"They have no intention of sharing their business interests so I wouldn't have thought they would spare you any of their free time."

"Don't be so hard on them, Ei."

"I'm sorry, but I cannot understand brothers or sisters who have no place for each other in the family's prosperity."

She knew she sounded bitter, but that was exactly how she felt.

"Well, anyway, you'd all better make the most of the next few weeks here and enjoy the country air while you have the chance."

"You haven't told me where the house is."

"You haven't asked, have you, wee wifey?"

"Is it near here?" Eileen didn't really expect that it would be, but perhaps there was a slight chance.

"It is on the road out from Glasgow, at any rate."

"Where exactly on the road. I expect you could say Gorbals was on the road from Glasgow to Eaglesham."

"You could, right enough. It is further out from the city than Gorbals, though. It is in Crosshill. Just across from the railway station in Cathcart Road."

"Oh, down that way" was all she allowed herself to comment.

Chapter 6

REPRIEVE

Gradually the village houses became unoccupied as new, modern ones were built elsewhere. People moved from the rural atmosphere, many choosing to live nearer their places of employment in the city and others settling for areas newly developed nearer Eaglesham.

Eileen and Tom took their family to larger premises in Cathcart Road, returning to Eaglesham only on visits. During one of these an old occupant of one of the smallest homes asked Tom, now the owner of his own building firm, if he could do anything to save the houses of the village from turning into slums.

Rising to the challenge, Tom interested the head of a joiner's business in the somewhat ambitious project of rehabilitating the derelict properties, knowing that when the Second World War ended soldiers and other servicemen would be desperately in need of homes.

Together, the two master tradesmen approached the appropriate council personnel and set out their scheme. They were laughed to scorn and told that the first thing to be done with Eaglesham when the war ended, was to take a bulldozer right down the two old streets. Red tape won and the two men eventually gave up the whole idea, with great reluctance.

The local householders were tired of their old homes, which had

*few conveniences, and most of them took kindly enough to being
rehoused in more modern ones.*

*One by one new people came on the scene, buying up the old
properties and putting them into shape for postwar living. Simul-
taneously, more and more houses were condemned, making the two
main streets look desolate and forlorn. The prospects for retaining the
old-new town of Eaglesham as the 10th Earl had envisaged it, and the
11th Earl had made it, looked bleak in the extreme.*

*   *   *

The first of the new areas of council-built houses was completed and
many of the families from the old village homes left Eaglesham and its
rural ways, for new lives in the start of the housing schemes.

Eileen thought it strange that some of them had no qualms about
doing so. They were more interested in the idea of living in a house
with modern fittings and amenities, especially bathrooms, than with
the particular area in which the house was actually built.

She had many misgivings about leaving the tiny place she had now
come to regard as home. Life in the quiet village, with its way of life
still much as it must have been in the days of the building of the Earl's
new town, was very pleasant. She did not expect that it would be so in
Cathcart Road, with the electric trams passing along only feet from their
front windows.

Acting on Tom's advice, she ensured that the children had as much
good from the countryside in their remaining days as was possible.

Some days were too cold to go very far afield, but on others she
dressed them warmly and set off with the two younger ones on walks
over moor and country roads, finding out all she could for her own
information. They always timed their return for the school children
coming out, and Jane accompanied them at the last lap.

Tom and some of his brothers were busy repairing and redecorating
the ground-flat house in the sandstone tenement building in Crosshill.
Eileen had felt she should be down with them, doing what she could
to help, but Tom had assured her she was doing her part in coping with
the children single-handed.

For the remaining weeks left to them of life in Eaglesham, she did
all she could to absorb the unique quality of life which the village
afforded them.

Some days found her deep in conversation with an old farmworker from one of the surrounding farms, others saw her investigating the little wild flowers which grew tucked away in sheltered corners and crevices, or studying the wild life of the woods around and in the village.

She listened eagerly to all the local stories repeated in one or other of the village's many little shops, either by the shopkeeper or one of the customers. Many tales were told by the older residents of their youthful days and Eileen found each one of them intensely interesting. Her imaginative and fertile mind found no difficulty in reconstructing the scenes which had been enacted in the very streets she walked and the selfsame buildings she entered almost daily.

Stories were many about the work which several of the older folks had been employed in at the mills. The largest employer of labour seemed to have been the biggest of the mills, the cotton spinning one, built on the Orry. Now it supplied nothing more than a good place for hide and seek to the village children, and a hazard to their safety at times, Eileen thought. One woman told her, with a world of pride in her old voice, that theirs had been the very first village to be lit by the new-fangled gas lighting.

Another had connections to a family who lived on the Gilmour's estate near Waterfoot, and could tell of life in the grand Eaglesham House which, probably because of its style of building, was more often than not referred to as "The Castle". She spoke of the fine exterior of the mansion house, and of the lovely finish to the woodwork of the main rooms, as well as of the extensive garden with its own wall-enclosed garden, its greenhouse with the vine, and its gardener's cottage and potting shed. She used to tell, also, of visits made to the families living in the two lodge houses, one on the Newton Mearns side of the estate and the other on the Eaglesham side, and to the coachman's house.

A favourite walk for the children visiting at the cottages, was to the memorial stone depicting an Iona cross which marked the burial spot of loved members of the Gilmour family.

The grandmother of one of Jane's school chums had a large and varied collection of old snapshots, and the children liked nothing better on a cold winter afternoon than to sit before the blazing fire in the old lady's tiny street-level home, which consisted of only a single square room, and listen to her as she told the story attached to each of her treasured pictures. Jane used to come home enthralled after these visits, and Eileen enjoyed hearing her accounts of such things as past means of transport. Apparently there were pictures of vehicles pulled by horses and referred to as horse-drawn buses, as well as more recent ones of motorised vehicles, with roll-down flaps on the sides. Jane liked the look of the older buses with their outside stair and open top to the upper deck, but Anna was more interested in the picture of the horses standing, unyoked and free from their burden, at the Inn awaiting the next journey. She was always insistent on relating the fact that there were hay stacks on the green behind the Inn.

Many residents remembered Mr. Picken of Polnoon who sold milk from his Park Farm and recited the poem written about it, which they considered as their poem, though the title was the "Soor Milk Cairt", referring to the buttermilk which the friendly farmer sold.

Sometimes Eileen took the children to the neighbouring village of Busby, with its big clock on the wall of the local branch of the "Co-op" store, and the ornate lamp standard with the shade bearing Dr. Russell's name, in the main street. Many happy hours they spent playing in the Busby Glen, when spring days brought warmer weather.

As she thought of the changes which living nearer the noise and grime of the city would bring, she questioned what the children would miss most. Would it be the fun they had enjoyed when playing with the other village children in the Orry and round the back closes and pends? Would it be the element of freedom which the rural setting of the village afforded, with its many farms and moors all around? Or would it be the times when the quiet of the usual evening hours was completely changed, and it seemed that the whole population of the village had taken to the streets.

That was when the snow had transformed the entire area into a sparkling, dazzling wonderland and every size and shape of home-made sledge was brought out from hiding under a boxbed, or high on the top shelf of a big cupboard, buried by an assortment of possessions more often used. What fun they all had, children and grown-ups alike, whizzing down the entire length of Montgomery Street, with the cold wind whistling against their ears and the excited shouts and laughter of the others ringing in them.

Whatever aspect they would miss most, Eileen knew that she herself would miss most of all the homely feel she always experienced as she walked with her children up the village street "in the gloaming", when the little paraffin lamps were lit and sent their cosy glow into the corners of all the village's homes, glimpsed through the low windows.

All too soon the Wallace family were forced to take their leave of Eaglesham and, without exception (apart from Billy who was too young to know what was going on), were filled with regret at having to do so.

* * *

The passage of time brings about many changes in the lives of most families and the Wallaces were no exception. A few years after they left their village home a third daughter was born.

Then Tom withdrew from the building industry, and his employment with his father, to enter the field of commerce. He was well equipped with what he himself called "the gift of the gab" and made good headway in the salesmanship world, finding ready sales for his company's electrical goods following the introduction of electricity into wide domestic use.

In 1930 Tom's father had acted very generously to Eileen, taking her with her newest daughter on a "round-the-world" cruise, together with his own wife and other members of his family. Eileen had appreciated it to the full, enjoying seeing all her own people and her country again after almost a decade.

As the years progressed, so did Tom's position in his firm; before long he became the area manager for a large section of Central Scotland's industrial zone. Altogether things were much more comfortable for Tom and Eileen, and therefore for their children. Until the blow which struck the whole of the western world, struck them also.

With the advent of "The War" in September of 1939, Tom lost his lucrative job almost overnight. Electrical equipment for the home, of which his company was one of the biggest manufacturers, had to go by the board so there was no further need for a sales force.

One of his younger brothers had broken away from the parent company some years previously and started a small building business on his own. Unfortunately, he had not lived long to enjoy being his own master and had left his widow the task of maintaining the new firm. Tom decided to re-enter the building industry which required older skilled tradesmen to replace all the younger ones who had been conscripted into the armed forces.

So he bought from his sister-in-law the little business his brother had established and settled down to the life of a slater once more.

Eileen had thought of sending their youngest child to safety in Australia when the British government were arranging the evacuation of school children. It had seemed too far to send the teenaged girl, although she had adapted well to the different climate and conditions there when, as a five-year-old, she had been taken out by her Grandfather; instead, Jo was sent to Kilmarnock—more for the purpose of obtaining steady schooling than to escape any German bombs.

After a few years of intensive hard slogging, Tom had managed to build up a thriving business which employed men of allied trades as well as his own trade. He had neither training nor inclination for the writing up of records or the keeping of books, which any such business requires.

He had already noted Jo's natural bent in that direction when he had enlisted her help with the large amount of bookwork necessary in the days when a team of salesmen worked under him with the electrical company. So when the time came for the girl to leave school, he sent her to College for a full secretarial training which would be of use in his business.

On the completion of this course Jo obtained a position in Glasgow with a large assurance company, but Tom made good use of his youngest daughter's abilities. After she returned home from the city office, he had her write up all his books and send out his accounts in the evenings.

Eileen had allowed things to go on thus for so long only; then she had stepped in. Either Jo worked for the assurance company—or she worked for Tom. Not for both!

By then, Tom had taken over new premises and he agreed to make part of them into an office where his daughter could carry out all the clerical side of his business. Jo's position with the city firm was terminated and she had taken her place as secretary of her father's thriving building firm. Tom and his young daughter worked long hours together, establishing and expanding the business and keeping their particular wheels running smoothly during the war years. As she was the firm's only office worker, Jo was not conscripted like some of her friends into the armed forces but was allowed to stay in Tom's business, now engaged in the important work of repairing bomb damage to schools and other public buildings.

Neither of Tom and Eileen's other daughters had been required to leave their positions, either. Jane was in a "reserved" Government post and Anna, by then happily married, was required by her employer as she was the head of a department.

Bill alone, their only son, had been called upon to leave home and serve his country on the high seas. Arriving home unannounced on unexpected leave one day, he had taken them all by surprise. Amid the excited greetings which followed, Eileen stood aside for a brief moment and breathed a silent prayer of thanksgiving for his safety.

Tom looked at him searchingly. "Some tan you've got! Been working —or lying on deck sunbathing, son?"

"Don't you worry. I've to work jolly hard. I enjoy my time ashore, though."

"My oath, I bet you do."

"Tom."

"Sorry, Ei."

Father and son exchanged winks and Jo, noticing, engaged her mother's attention.

When Jane came home from the office in College Street, one of Glasgow's oldest areas, and they were all seated at the big round table, with its carved central leg splaying into three with elaborate dragons' heads at the end of each, Tom told them of an incident in his day.

"Do you know who I met this morning? Old Sannie."

"Who?"

"Remember, Ei. The old joiner who lived over the green in Eaglesham."

"Yes. I remember him, Dad. He used to pull my hair."

"That's the one, Jane. Well, he says a lot of the old houses up there are falling to bits and nobody is doing anything about it."

"Well, I suppose they weren't allowed to spend any money on them. I'm sure the £10 a year which the government allows, wouldn't be enough. Some of them were pretty badly in need of repair, even when we lived there."

"I can't remember that. How long ago is it?"

"No wonder you can't. You were still in a pushchair."

"And Jo wasn't even thought of, was she, Ei?"

"I always think that Eaglesham was the best place we ever lived in. I still like it." Jane was unusually emphatic.

"I don't think I've ever been there."

"Oh, yes, you have, Jo. Your Mum and I often used to take you there on a warm evening when you were small."

"That was before petrol was rationed." Eileen laughed.

"Oh, long before that. She couldn't have been very old because I remember we always had a bother making her leave the swings to come home."

"Is that the place with the big park on a hill, and a burn in it?"

"That's right, Bill. You probably used to come with us sometimes, too."

"Yes, he did. I remember he used to play football with other boys in the "Orry" while I pushed Jo on the swings."

"I suppose Jane is quite right. We did enjoy Eaglesham, both when we lived there and when we used to take the younger ones to play there later. I wonder."

Eileen looked across the table at Tom's face but couldn't tell from his expression what made him wonder.

"Come on then, Dad. Tell us what you wonder."

"Well, son, I wonder whether I could do anything to save those old houses. We all owe a big debt to Eaglesham."

"How would you go about that?" Bill was studying his father intently, and Eileen tried to read his thoughts, too.

"Remind me about it in the office tomorrow, Jo. I think I will have a word with Stewart about approaching the County Council."

"Why them? I thought all the houses were private property." Eileen remembered how the villagers used to be so proud of owning their homes, both small and larger ones.

"They were—till they became so delapidated that some of their owners were glad to let the Council take them off their hands."

"What a pity. I used to think of all the hopes and dreams which the men who built them, must have woven into their walls."

"That's right. I remember you used to sit for hours on end writing all about old Eaglesham. Where are those old notebooks now, Ei?" Tom was enjoying teasing her, as he always did, but she would not be coaxed to reveal the whereabouts of her closely-written pages.

* * *

"Remember you are to go to Paisley this afternoon, Dad."

Jo did not lift her eyes from the closely worded specification which she was typing in her father's office. When she received no reply from

91

him she stopped what she was doing, swivelled round in her chair and looked at the corpulent figure seated at a second desk.

"You haven't remembered, have you?"

"I'm just trying to think whereabouts in Paisley it is I have to go."

"Now don't try to fool me. You know quite well that you haven't the slightest notion of where you are to go—or whom you have to see, for that matter."

"I just leave all these things to you, Jo. You always keep me right."

"It's just as well. You are going with the joiner. . . ." She did not manage to finish the sentence.

"That's it. We are to meet the Renfrewshire County Council men at the County Buildings. I didn't forget, you see."

Jo laughed indulgently at the satisfied smugness.

"Do you think you will be allowed to repair the old houses in Eaglesham?"

He took off his heavy horn-rimmed spectacles and slowly laid them down on top of the bundle of papers he had been reading.

"I don't really know. Local authorities are a bit tricky to deal with. Very often their members have good reasons of their own to allocate work to chosen firms. It has been known for some in other counties to demolish perfectly good property and build atrocities, which nobody either wanted or appreciated, on the sites, simply to provide contracts for chosen firms."

"You mean that they may decide to pull down the old houses."

"They could well do just that, though I hope they don't. Eaglesham has always been a favourite place for Glasgow folk. When I was a wee nipper my father used to take us out there, and we played football in our bare feet on the big green. We made up a good five-a-side, the eight of us with the old man and old Uncle Jimmie."

"Did Grandpa and Uncle Jimmie Welsh play in bare feet?" Jo couldn't keep the astonishment from her voice.

"No. They didn't. But my brothers and I all did."

"Didn't it hurt?"

"Hurt? Never! We were used to it. We played about the back courts in Oatlands, among the gravel and broken glass and such like, in our bare feet. Eaglesham's grass was like velvet to our soles." He laughed at his own humour. Then, as though reliving those carefree days, he started to sing some of the old jingles which he must often have chanted in the back yards:

"Queen Mary, Queen Mary, my age is sixteen,
My faither's a feirmer on yonder green,
Wi' plenty o' money to dress me fu' braw,
But nae bonnie laddie will tak' me awa'!"

"Somehow Eaglesham has always seemed like a different world to me; in the same way as Australia does. Perhaps it's because I was not alive when you all stayed in both places."

"You did stay in Australia when you were a wee thing."

"Oh, but that was only for a short time. It was really just a holiday."

"Well I can assure you that Eaglesham and Australia are very different worlds."

"Are you ever sorry you left Australia and came back home to Scotland again, Dad?"

"I've never ceased to be sorry" was all he answered, but Jo knew, by the determined way in which he rose, pushed back his chair, lifted his "Anthony Eden" felt hat from a nearby hook and rammed it on his shiny bald head, how vehemently he felt it.

She turned back to her typewriter and resumed her work without further comment. She was quite used to her father suddenly leaving the office and disappearing for hours on end, so thought nothing of it when she didn't see him again till after four o'clock.

"Well, that was one big waste of time, I can tell you."

Jo hadn't realised that he had been away from the office sufficient time to reach Paisley, have the interview with the Council personnel and be back again.

"What was?"

The hat was rammed on to the hook this time and her father very deliberately framed his reply, hissing out each word.

"Approaching the gentlemen of Renfrewshire County Council re the rehabilitating of Eaglesham village houses."

"You mean they wouldn't agree to your proposals?"

"I mean they laughed in our faces."

"Oh, Dad. What did you say?"

"I told them that all the boys coming home from the war would be glad to have a wee house that had been repaired."

"And they?"

"Said the first thing to be done with Eaglesham was take one of those newfangled automobile demolishers down one street and up the other."

"You mean bulldozer," she supplied.

"Whatever they are called, then. Fancy them knocking down the whole wee place. They'll probably build housing scheme property all round the village green—if not on it."

"Well, never mind. You tried."

"Aye, but I didn't succeed, did I? Trying is not enough. Make me a cup of tea, will you, then I'll catch a bus up there. Don't wait for me, just lock up and go home at five o'clock."

"When will you be home for tea?"

"Just tell your Mum I'm away to try and save some of old Eaglesham. She'll be so pleased to hear it, that she won't bother about not knowing when I'll be home for tea."

Jo knew better than to argue with her father when he had that look on his face. She would explain to her mother when she arrived home.

It was a good three hours later when she heard her father's step on the front path.

"Here's Dad now, Mum."

"I've kept his meal hot in the oven. Sit still, Jo, I'll see to it."

"You'll be tired, I'll get it for him."

Eileen watched her "baby" and thought how attentive she was to Tom. Her thoughts went back to the time in Cathcart Road when she first discovered that another child was on the way. They were having a hard enough struggle to keep three children, and she was distressed to learn she was to have a fourth.

She remembered how upset she had been when at length she had to consult their kindly doctor, Dr. Murdoch. She never could pronounce his name properly, making it sound like Mirdock, the children always told her. Tom had insisted she see him, even accompanying her to the surgery door to make sure she did. When she entered the consulting room she was full of resentment at the forthcoming event. When she left it, she had tears of mortification in her eyes.

Tom had asked her on the way home why she was upset and she had told him. Old Dr. Murdoch had seen her resentment over the new life soon to make its advent and had rebuked her in a quiet way, by saying "I can take you to an excellent lady who would give everything she owned to be in your shoes. You should be thanking God for an added blessing."

Now, almost twenty years later, she was reaping the full benefit of that blessing, as she had done from all her children before, and humiliation possessed her.

When Tom had finished eating, he brought his cup of tea over to the fireside and sat down in a nearby chair.

"You wouldn't recognise some of the old houses up in Montgomery Street today, Ei."

"Are they as bad as that?"

"It's a perishing shame. Some of those houses could be made really nice with not too much being spent on them."

"You mean that the Council aren't willing to spend money on them?"

"They want to pull the lot down."

"Oh, no, not Eaglesham. It's got a charm all its own."

"Not so much now, Ei. Certainly one or two have been modernised and look quite nice. It's new folk that have done them up, though."

"What about the people who lived there for years?"

"Some of them can't get out of the old places quick enough. They want new council houses with "all mod. cons.". One woman told me she knew of at least two others who had thrown buckets of water on the inside walls to make them appear damp when the inspector came."

"I think they are quite right to want modern homes in this day and age. I hope that when I get married I'll not need to go into a house with no bathroom or hot water."

"If you can get a house at all, Jo, you'll be lucky. Folks with families will come first."

"Well, Mum, I won't marry till I do."

"Don't talk like that. It's tempting providence."

"Well, Eaglesham is a pretty forlorn place these days, with its front street windows boarded up and its back buildings falling to pieces."

"I wonder what the Earl who planned it, or his brother who watched over its building, would think of it now."

"Not much, I warrant."

They all fell silent; suddenly a gloomy shadow seemed to have entered the bright room and settled on each of its occupants.

Eileen resented it and made a positive effort to dispel its ill effects.

"Perhaps someone, some day, will do something to secure Eaglesham's survival." She pronounced each word distinctly, stressing every "s" as though to impress their meaning on the haunting gloomy presence.

"We can only hope so . . . though I doubt it myself."

"You're a true namesake of the doubter, Thomas."

11. Polnoon Lodge after restoration

12 The Mid Road Bridge and Polnoon Street now

Chapter 7

REHABILITATION

Although the old folk with whom Eileen and her family had kept in touch were gone, Tom often drove his wife out to the village and together they watched the changes take place. The three children whom they had played with on the green grass of the common were now all grown adults. The last of their family, who had been born after they left Eaglesham, was now a married woman with two young daughters of her own.

On a summer afternoon early in 1959, Eileen and Tom sat on one of the seats in the "Orry". Nearby a villager played with two of her grandchildren. She heard Eileen speak and had a feeling that she should know the voice. As she played with the children, she watched and listened. Sensing that someone was observing her, Eileen's attention was caught by the little group and she remarked to Tom that they recalled days when she had played on the same spot with her own children, soon after they arrived from Australia. At the mention of Australia the other woman's recollections crystallised. It transpired that she had been their landlady when they lived in Eaglesham and she invited them to her new council house for a meal. From her they learned the story of the formation of the Preservation Society, the Resident's Association and the Restoration Joint Committee.

Soon after, Eileen, whose health had been poor for several years, was

*taken to hospital and after some weeks of concern, died there. At her
funeral in the little cemetery in nearby Mearns, a relative recalled his
first meeting with her, in Eaglesham. He told of friends who had bought
one of the old properties and were busy putting it into shape, and
suggested to Eileen's son-in-law that it would be a good idea for him
to do likewise; he did not agree, though.*

*　　*　　*

Eileen was not well. She had been struggling hard to convince herself
that she was fine, but by early afternoon she knew she was only kidding
herself. It was nearly ten years since the family doctor, who had been
their medical adviser ever since old Dr. Murdoch died, broke it gently to
her that she had contracted a malady for which they had no cure.

At fairly frequent intervals since that day, she had been kept for
varying lengths of time in hospitals. Mostly she had been in the nearest,
the Victoria Infirmary, sometimes landing out at Philipshill to con-
valesce, but when there were special tests, or observations, to be carried
out, she was taken into the city's Western Infirmary.

Whenever anyone asked her how she was feeling, she purposely
answered "Fine" and gave a sad little smile. She knew quite well that
she would never again be "fine", but what was the use of burdening
other folk with her complaints and causing them any sadness on her
behalf. She reckoned they would all have plenty worries of their own.

In spite of her valiant efforts to keep on the go, she was forced to
stop and lie down for a bit. Although she felt severe pain, she somehow
also felt her consciousness rise up as though transcending and super-
ceding the pain. Deep within her she knew perfect serenity.

As she lay motionless, yet wide-eyed, on top of the big bed her
thoughts travelled back down the years. She was now living on borrowed
time, having reached her "three score years and ten" the previous year.

Looking back, she acknowledged that she had known better material
blessings and certainly more personal happiness, than many others
whom she knew. Her heart lifted in silent thanksgiving. All in all, she
had no cause for complaint; life had not been too rough with her.
Apart from the blood condition which had resulted in her developing
leukemia, none of them had ever known what it was to have broken or ill
health. Certainly there were times when minor illnesses had caused both
Tom and herself some concern, but they had always been short lived.

As she thought of all the unemployment and depression which had existed in the years between the wars, and the times when workers in differing fields had known slackness, she appreciated that her husband was one of those who turned his hand to whatever he could find to do, in order to provide for his family. Often he had remarked to her "Don't worry about the future, Ei. When one door shuts another one will open, never fear."

Now they could look at their son and daughters, all comfortable and healthy, and feel a sense of achievement and satisfaction. In addition, they now had a grandson and three grand-daughters.

Many changes had taken place in the world during her lifetime and she thought of some of them as beneficial and others as the reverse. So preoccupied was she, that she had not heard Tom's car draw up outside their old villa near the Hampden Football Ground.

When he walked into the room, she was quite startled.

"Hello. This is a funny time for you to come home."

"I just thought I'd take the afternoon to myself as it is so warm. Are you not feeling so good?"

"I felt a bit queer, but I'm a bit better now."

"Would you like a wee spin somewhere in the car?"

"Oh, I don't know."

She didn't want any such thing, but did not wish to hurt his feelings by saying so, outright.

"I thought we could take a turn down to Largs and have a meal there."

She could see that he was in the mood for a drive and would be disappointed if she didn't agree.

"I think that would be a longer run than I could go today, Tom."

She could tell that her words shook him.

"You are not well, then, Ei. You can usually go any distance without even turning a hair."

"That's right. Perhaps I could manage it." She hated not fitting in with his wishes; probably because she had always done so.

"You'll feel better once you are out in the sunshine."

He proved to be quite wrong. They were not long in the car when she began to feel unwell again, and though she tried to hide what she was suffering, Tom noticed.

"I don't think you really want to go to Largs, do you? We'll just turn off here and go home again."

99

"But you wanted an outing. Maybe you could go to Eaglesham or somewhere near at hand and I'll sit in the car?"

Without replying, he turned the car sharply off the Largs road and headed in a different direction. Eileen could sense his disappointment. It was not very often he took time off from his business; he would not do so again in a hurry, she guessed.

As they approached it, Eaglesham lay bathed in the full blaze of the June sunshine. Almost immediately, Eileen felt her spirits lift.

"Drive on to the Mid road and we can have a seat in the 'Orry'."

"Are you sure you are all right?" She detected the anxiety in his tone and wondered whether he, too, guessed that all was not well. Not wishing him to have any suspicions confirmed, she hurried to assure him that she would be "Fine".

"You always say that, whether you feel it or not."

She only gave one of her rare little laughs.

They sat enjoying the sun for quite a time, before either of them spoke. Dotted throughout the green slopes of the Orry, were groups of children either with or without adult companions. Close to where they sat a woman of about Eileen's own age played with two children.

"I'm just looking at the way that woman is enjoying those kids' fun, Ei."

"Yes, so am I."

"Do you ever wish that Jo and her two wee ones lived nearer?"

"Oh, I'm quite happy to see them some time every week. Sometimes I wish they still lived in Govanhill. Sometimes I'm quite glad to see them go home to Cardonald though." She gave her twisted little smile. "I'm not as young as I used to be."

They sat on in silence, each nursing private thoughts. Eileen knew that Tom had been disappointed when Jo had married and started her own family; he had hoped she would stay with him in the business. When he first took her from her position with a big assurance company in Glasgow, to help him build up business in the new premises he bought on the Clarkston Road, he had great plans. He told the young girl she would have shares in the firm and that it was in her own interest to work as hard as she knew how. Eileen remembered how literally her youngest daughter carried out Tom's advice. Repeatedly she herself had to tell the girl to slow down a bit and stop trying to do the impossible. Somehow, the more work there was to be done, the greater seemed to be the challenge to Jo. She thought of one night in particular when Tom had told her how much work the teenaged youngster had successfully completed during that day. He had been so proud of her.

Although neither of them had any objection to her choice of husband, Tom had been quite blunt about her even wanting one. "Why can't you stay single and let your sister get married?" he had asked, without stopping to think how much he might hurt her. Jo was sensitive, like herself, and Eileen had known something of the wound his words had inflicted. She had always thought it strange that the last of her children, the one whom she had not really wanted at all, was the one to inherit much of her own nature. Almost as though it was meant that the child should be born to perpetuate herself.

As Eileen's thoughts traversed down the years she recalled the days when she, like the woman nearby, sat and watched her children at play on the selfsame spot. Sometimes she had joined in their games. Jane was then a curly-haired, alert child . . . now she was a middle-aged career woman, occupying a responsible executive position in a Government office. Anna had been a live wire, just coming up to school age and Bill had only been a baby learning to walk.

Although her thoughts were far from the present, she was nonetheless aware of the attention the woman with the children was paying her.

"No, neither of us are." Tom's voice recalled her to the present and she had to make a mental effort to remember what they had been speaking about. Then she did remember.

"Yet it doesn't seem all that long ago since we played about here with our own children. Now we are discussing Jo's girls, and Jo wasn't even born then."

"Aye. That's life. I wonder what they would all be doing now, if I had never brought you here from Australia."

"There's no saying. I don't suppose there's any point in even thinking about that."

Eileen noticed that the other woman was actually listening to their conversation by this time. Then she walked towards the seat which they were occupying and Eileen was surprised when she spoke.

"Excuse me. I hope you don't think I'm very rude, but I have been trying to place you since you sat down. It wasn't till I heard 'Australia' that I managed, though."

All the time she was speaking Eileen racked her brain in an effort to identify her, but without avail.

101

"Aren't you Jane and Anna's parents?" she pursued.

In a very short time, they were all chatting together about the days when the Wallace family lived in the tiny room-and-kitchen home in Montgomery Street and the unrecognised woman was their landlady. Mrs. Smith now had a new council house in Eaglesham and seemed so keen for them to join her there for tea, that Eileen did not have the heart to plead her lack of good health, for fear of causing offence.

After duly admiring the new home and partaking of their hostess's well-cooked meal, Tom told her of the approach he had made to the Council about restoring the old properties and the response with which his suggestion had been met.

"It seems a shame to demolish the little village. I'll never forget the initial effect it had on me. In fact, I was so interested in it and it's history when I lived in your wee house, that I wrote all about it in old notebooks."

"They're not going to demolish it, though, after all."

"Are you sure?" Tom didn't sound as though he was, anyway, Eileen thought.

"Positive."

"Then are they going to repair the old buildings?"

"The Council are not, if that's what you mean."

"Then who is?"

Like a flash, Eileen thought of the family who had once owned and taken a pride in their model village.

"Are the members of the Eglinton family stepping in to save it?"

"Which family are they?"

"The Earls of Eglinton who built the village."

"Oh, I see. No. It's ordinary people, who are buying the old places as they stand and modernising them for their own homes. Some of them belong to Eaglesham but a lot are coming in from Glasgow and other places."

"I am glad. It would have been such a pity to lose the old place. It has always had a special charm all of its own."

"So long as you didn't have to light paraffin lamps when other folk had electricity for lighting and cooking, or draw water from an old outdoor pump and heat it on the fire. Believe me, those of us who lived that way for so long were only too glad to be given the chance of electricity and hot water laid on, with a proper bathroom in our houses instead of only a water closet outside."

"I suppose so. Mind you, that's what I was used to as well in my childhood."

"Yes, but you were glad to wash in cold water to cool you down, Ei."

"That's true."

"It was no fun here in some of the worst of the old places, especially those with damp walls, in a cold winter. Those were the first ones to be vacated and their occupants given new houses."

"Do you think the new folks who will be renovating the old properties will spoil the village's appearance. I mean, will they start and introduce all kinds of modern buildings and take away its uniformity?"

"They won't be allowed to do that. We have our own Preservation Society, as well as a more usual Resident's Association. Then we have also our Restoration Joint Committee."

"My. You are quite a place, now, aren't you?"

"Oh, yes. Since a few years back now. A few of the old residents, and also of the new, got together and formed a Preservation Society, enlisting over 200 members by the time they held the first meeting about three years ago. The Earl of Eglinton agreed to their proposal that he become President. They interested the Secretary of State, the National Trust, the County Council and I don't know who all."

"Very good."

"Oh, that was only a beginning. One by one, the old properties were

103

bought up and either new ones were erected on the sites (having to adhere rigidly to rules of building) or the old ones were completely renovated and restored. Then a Resident's Association was formed, largely under the guidance of our Councillor, then soon after another committee was decided on, to tie up all the efforts of the others, as it were. That was called The Restoration Joint Committee and I think that it will be the main factor in the village's future."

After another few minutes of exchanging news and views, when Mrs. Smith told them of her children's and grandchildren's whereabouts and learned about those of the family to whom she had "let out" her holiday house higher up Montgomery Street than her own, Tom recalled his first meeting with her.

"Do you remember that day when I came to ask you to 'let' us your place?"

"I remember it fine. You never even looked at it."

"That's right. When Eileen asked me what kind of a house it was that I'd found in Eaglesham, I didn't even know."

"Tom!"

"That's right. You never knew that before, did you?"

"I certainly did not. What if it had been a dirty place, or even verminous like the ones you used to tell us about in Gorbals and Tradeston?" She was utterly appalled.

Mrs. Smith laughed. "I remember when I asked him if he didn't even want to see it, he only looked me up and down, then looked at my own place and said, 'It'll do. I can see you are clean'." She laughed again at the recollection of it.

"I am certainly glad that you were. I shudder to think what would have happened if you were not."

"You would simply have set to and made it so, Ei. Think of the mess we had to sort out in the Cathcart Road house, after we left Mrs. Smith's."

She smiled wryly as she answered, "I'd rather not, thank you. Between dirt and beetles, it was a bit of a nightmare."

*   *   *

Later that summer Eileen's health deteriorated rapidly and she had been taken once more into the same ward in Glasgow's Victoria Infirmary where she had been on several previous occasions.

Within herself, though she did not wish Tom or any of her children to guess the truth, she knew that she would not leave its confines again in the flesh. She comforted herself, as she had done many poor souls in the same place in the past, that when her sickly body at last gave up the fight, her spirit would go free and return unhampered to its Creator.

Tom was bending over the snowy-white bed, looking anxiously into her eyes, and fumbling clumsily for words of comfort. Poor Tom, she thought, he surely is out of his depths here. Was there no one else come to visit her, she wondered wearily. Then she sunk back into semi-consciousness, mid-way between heaven and earth it seemed, and only stirred out of it when she heard her husband addressing someone coming up the ward.

"I don't think your mother's too good today. She won't speak to me at all. She only said a few words when I first came in, then looked at me without answering when I spoke to her."

"Let me speak to her, Dad. Here, you take the baby and let me over there."

Jo handed her plump little toddler across the bed to her father, but before he could take his grand-daughter Eileen roused herself with a tremendous struggle. "Give her to me." The wavering voice was like that of a stranger.

She pulled herself up on to her pillows and put out both her pitifully thin arms to hold the little girl. She saw the look of incredulity which Jo exchanged with her father.

"What a pretty pink dress."

"Yes, isn't it, Gran. Her Uncle Bill bought her that one."

"It's lovely. Just like its little wearer." Then she lifted the child high above her head and looked for a long, long minute at the healthy features and tightly-curled mop of fair hair.

"Take her, Jo," was all she managed before her strength disappeared and she sank back into the pillows. She lay quite motionless for a little and neither her husband nor her daughter seemed to know whether to speak to her or not.

She felt sorry for them sitting there. Tom on one side of her bed, with a lost frightened kind of expression, and Jo on the other, with the bouncing toddler, so full of life, jumping up and down on her lap. Life and death side by side, she thought.

The big round clock high on the far wall of the ward ticked the minutes away, but still neither Tom nor Jo spoke. The infant fidgeted about impatiently on her mother's knee and Eileen could see that Jo was finding it difficult to keep her little girl good.

She made one last effort at conversation.

"It's good to see you. I was very ill last night and didn't expect ever to see any of you again." It was the first time she had admitted her knowledge of the extent of her illness. She hadn't meant to do so, but it came to her lips unbidden.

"Don't talk like that, Mum. You'll be all right again soon, the same as you are every time."

Eileen gave her a long, searching stare. Jo, her baby, had always been very near to her and they had an indefinable affinity which afforded them a total trust one for the other. She let her eyes search her daughter's, until she became aware that the latter had interpreted her thoughts. She might have expected anyone else to endeavour to reassure her, though knowing it to be in vain. Not Jo, though. She had to show her that she was not fooled by the remark.

Jo flinched beneath her gaze and caught her breath on a stifled sob before she bent her head over the smaller one of her child.

Tom was looking on helplessly. He didn't seem to believe his own ears or eyes. She raised one of her hands rather shakily in his direction and he gripped it in both of his till it hurt. She closed her eyes against the pain.

"Do you feel much pain, Mum."

Jo must have seen the pain in her face and mistaken it for inward pain. She must reassure her, now.

"No. No pain at all. Only a terrible weakness." So much, she told herself, that I can't go on any longer.

"That's good then. I think I'll go now, Mum."

Then Eileen knew that Jo had read her unspoken words. The message had reached her; she had communicated to her daughter that she knew just what was what. Now she, in turn, was letting her know that she understood also.

Eileen was content.

Jo and the child both kissed her lovingly, then Jo lifted a large bunch of multi-hued sweet peas and gently placed it in her hands, now lying limply on top of the bedclothes.

"That's the very last of them. I stripped the row for you." She looked long and searchingly again into her eyes.

As she watched her youngest child and grandchild move away from her down the long stretch of the ward, she lifted the sweet-smelling blooms and buried her face in them. When she looked up again she saw Tom wipe the corner of his eyes. Poor Tom, she thought, I wonder how he will do without me. Then she felt herself drifting further and further away from him.

* * *

Although it was into September, the sun's rays were still warm on the large group of mourners who made their way back to the waiting cars at the gateway.

Tom's shiny bald head was bowed above his black jacket and striped trousers. Various relatives were walking beside and behind him, among them a brother-in-law and Jo's husband. Although it was Eileen's funeral, none of her own kith and kin attended. She was far removed from all her own, in death as she had been for so long in her life.

He thought of the big step they took when they mounted the gangway on to the huge liner in Sydney, so many years ago. As if in line with his thoughts he heard his brother-in-law recounting to Jo's young husband the first meeting he had with Eileen.

"They were living in a house of sorts not far from Mearns here. Eaglesham, actually. I remember Jimmie, Tom's brother, was there too. He introduced me to her, in fact, by leaning his elbow on her shoulder

107

and saying 'This is Eileen—I lean on Eileen.' He seemed to think that was quite a joke."

The talk went from Eileen to Eaglesham and of the old properties there. Most of the listeners were quite familiar with the village and became interested in hearing of how some of the old places were being renovated.

"Would you not think of buying one of them, Alex?"

"Me?"

"Yes. I'm sure Jo and the children would love to live in Eaglesham. It has such healthy air."

"Thanks, but I'd sooner give them a good home in Cardonald without the healthy air, than a slum in Eaglesham with it."

Chapter 8

RETURN

Several years after Eileen's death her youngest daughter, Jo, with her husband and two girls, moved house to the Cathcart district of Glasgow. When there, she became interested in the village to which her mother was taken to live soon after her arrival from Australia. In her turn she also became intrigued by the atmosphere of it and set about learning more of Eaglesham.

In 1969 the bi-centenary of the founding of the village was celebrated with due style and festivities. The public hall—Montgomery Hall—was the scene of a floral art exhibition and the newly restored Polnoon Lodge, once the Earls' Hunting Lodge, was opened to public viewing showing the transformation of the old building into modern homes for local old age pensioners. Amid all the excitement of pageantry, processions, and the like, the charming young Countess of Eglinton and Winton officiated at the crowning of the "village queen" on the lower grass of the old village common, one of the first pieces of land owned by one of the first members of that long line of landowners in Scotland.

Among the large crowd of villagers and visitors who attended the "coronation" was Eileen's daughter and two grand-daughters. As they journeyed home by car to Cathcart later in the day, the talk turned to

Eaglesham as being one of the first places where their own family had put down roots almost half a century before.

*   *   *

Almost ten years had passed since Eileen's death and Jo had moved house from Cardonald to Cathcart.

She had been very happy in Cardonald as had Alex and their two daughters, for about eight years. Then she felt that she would like to be nearer her father who had taken a sudden attack at business one day, causing Jane and Anna quite a bit of concern. It was something that not one of them could believe; Tom had always had perfect health and somehow his daughters had not reckoned on it ever ceasing.

In addition, their brother's wife had taken very ill and was completely helpless for several months. Bill rose to the occasion admirably, but Anna liked to give all the help she could. Between father and sister-in-law she was kept hard at it. Life had dealt somewhat harshly with her, robbing her of her young husband and leaving their four-year-old son fatherless, after only a few years of marriage. Even so, Anna was always the first person with practical help in the time of anyone's need.

Feeling that the heavy end of the stick was resting on her sister yet again, Jo persuaded her husband to sell their home in Cardonald and buy one nearby the old villa which had been Eileen's last home, and where the other family members still lived.

The winter had long gone and spring was also a thing of the past. One forenoon during April, Jo had taken one of her Cardonald friends to Eaglesham, where they had morning tea in the Wishing Well Tearoom. Her friend had never been in the village before and was completely captivated by its old-world charm. She asked Jo how she came to know about it and was very interested to learn that her parents had come to live in one of the village houses nearly fifty years earlier.

Since that forenoon, Jo had spent many happy hours in the village, drinking in its restful atmosphere and revelling in its unique charm, in much the same way as her mother had done. She had read notices in more than one of its shops intimating the village's forthcoming Fair and Celebrations to mark its Bi-centenary on a Saturday in May. The date was Alex's birthday so she had not experienced any difficulty in remembering it.

The summer had come early and the weather was really warm on the day before the Fair.

Alex had a day off from his work and together they had driven to collect bedding plants from a nurseryman in Chapelton.

"What do you say, that we carry on to Strathaven for a cup of coffee, then go to Hamilton and bring Dianne home for the week-end."

"That's a good idea, Alex. It's a lovely day and probably too hot to bed out the plants until the evening."

"I'm going to Hampden tomorrow, so we won't be able to have a run then."

"Oh, that's good."

"Now what exactly do you mean by that remark, may I ask?"

Jo laughed. "I suppose it did sound funny. I mean it's good that you won't be wanting my company tomorrow, because I want to go to Eaglesham."

"Oh, no," he groaned. "Not again. You should live there, Jo. You'd save yourself the travelling time."

"I'd love to live there. Why don't we put our name down for one of the new houses they are building?"

"No, thank you. I've told you for years that I have no desire to stay in Eaglesham."

"I know you have, but that was when it was falling to bits."

"Isn't it still?"

"You know quite well it isn't."

"I know I'm not going to buy a house there."

"Oh, don't then. One day I'll buy one myself."

He laughed at the very idea.

"Are you going househunting tomorrow, then?"

She knew that he was deliberately goading her, for the sheer fun of seeing her anger rise, so she just as deliberately chose to remain silent—though she knew he would also laugh at her if she continued the silence for long.

After failing to receive any reply from her to several more remarks, he switched on the radio and kept it on until he swung the big saloon through the iron gates which had once led in to the Duke of Hamilton's palace—and were now the entrance to the Hamilton College of Education, built in the old palace grounds.

"You think Dianne looks a fright sometimes. Take a look at this lot."

Jo had at last to break her stupid silence, to agree with him that their daughter at least looked a good deal tidier than many of the young students walking up the driveways from one or other of the Halls of Residence.

They were just turning in to the little parking bay in front of her particular building, Cadzow Hall, when they spotted her coming through the glass-fronted hallway. She saw the car turning and gave a cheery smile as she hurried out through the door, case in hand.

"Hullo," she greeted them with her impish grin. "That was nice of you to come and collect me. I hate having to come by bus."

Her father hated to give the impression that he had gone out of his way for her convenience. "We were out, anyway, and not far from here," he hastened to inform her.

Jo noted, with appreciation, that her daughter had sought to rectify the bad impression she had created on a previous week-end at home, when she had arrived looking like a tramp with tatty denim trousers carefully frayed into ribbons at the bottom and her lovely fair hair, cropped of all its natural wave and curl, looking like a street urchin of past days.

"You are looking very nice," she told her.

It was no more than the truth for Dianne was wearing a dress of sky blue material, striped with narrow rust and yellow bands, and had hidden her urchin haircut by donning a wig of straight, straw-coloured shoulder-length "nylon hair" and a hairband of matching blue covered the telltale join where wig and hair met.

"Thanks, Mum." She sounded surprised, almost as though she never expected to be complimented on anything by her, thought Jo.

On the way home they discussed, among other things, their respective plans for the week-end. Dianne was not surprised to learn that her father would be attending the football match in Hampden Park on the Saturday; nor was she surprised to learn that her mother would be visiting Eaglesham. Neither event was out of the ordinary. She was both interested and surprised, though, to learn that her mother had good cause to visit Eaglesham that week-end.

"You mean they will hold a real village fair?" she asked.

"That's what I expect, anyway. At least it will be some kind of special

13. Millhall after restoration

14.   Church and Churchyard, now

celebration to mark the bi-centenary of the founding of the re-styled Eaglesham."

"I'm not doing anything special; perhaps I'll come with you."

*　　*　　*

Both Jo's daughters accompanied her to the Bi-centenary celebrations in Eaglesham on a warm Saturday in May of 1969. After they had watched the various decorated floats drive in procession along the main streets they joined in the "fun of the fair" on the lower grass and formed part of the crowd surrounding the outdoor stage where the "crowning of the village queen" ceremony took place.

As it was a very special occasion to all the people of the Renfrewshire village, those arranging the proceedings had taken the bold step of approaching the 18th Earl of Eglinton and Winton to request his presence, with that of his Countess, at their great day's activities.

Polnoon Lodge, originally the hunting lodge built and used by a fore-bear of the Earl, had long since lost its glory. Among other uses since the days of hunting in the area, it had known existence as a boarding house, but more recently it had fast been falling into a ruinous state, like much of the village property. Then it was decided to restore the fine old building situated to the north-east of Gilmour Street, and utilise it as housing accommodation for elderly persons. Local shopkeepers and others had been called upon to decorate and furnish the newly-restored building for the celebration period, and it was on view to all—including the Earl and Countess.

Another old property had been renovated and put to a new use at the same time as Polnoon Lodge; it, too, was completed in time for the village's bi-centenary. High up Montgomery Street a treasure chest had been opened up within the fabric of an old residence, revealing items and objects carefully preserved from distant days. In honour of the return visit to Eaglesham by a descendant of its worthy founder, the owner of The Treasure Chest had adorned its interior with drapings of Montgomery tartan and displays of emblems symbolic of the Montgom-ery family. Both the Earl and Countess were thrilled at this authentic touch and were delighted when they were presented with a dainty antique pillbox by the treasure chest's owner, the local antique dealer.

As the handsome Earl and his charming young Countess toured the village and inspected some of its old properties, Jo thought about the changes which must have taken place in it since the 8th Earl, Alexander, first sought authority to hold an annual fair in the far-off days of King Charles II. Or even the changes which the years had wrought since a much more recent Earl of Eglinton envisaged the making of a presentable road from the village to his Cleuchearn estate, in the uplands of East Kilbride, on which he could drive when travelling between his country estate of Cleuchearn and his residence of Eglinton Castle, a twenty-mile stretch, without leaving his own land. Had it not been for the lavish outlay of funds during the four-day attempt to revive the ancient glories of chivalry, with the famous Eglinton Tournament one hundred and thirty years previously, such a road traversing lands and estates still in the possession of an Earl of Eglinton might exist.

Jo had borrowed her husband's new camera, hoping to obtain better photographs with it than she could have done with her old, cheap one. Much to her annoyance, though, its shutter control had jammed and she failed in all her attempts to operate it.

"Let's go and see the crowning of the Village Queen before we go home," she suggested.

There was quite a large crowd already surrounding the wooden structure which had been erected on the green at the foot of the village, so Jo had to lift her younger daughter in her arms to let her see the queen and her maidens seated amid local dignitaries.

"If you give me Dad's camera, I'll try taking a picture," Dianne offered.

"I hope you succeed," was all her mother answered as she handed it over.

There was an excited stir in the crowd as word passed around that the Earl and the Countess were approaching and soon they were seated atop the wooden stage. Jo could see Dianne frantically endeavouring to make Alex's camera operate, but she feared that, although the girl had managed to find a good stance near the platform, they would not have any photographic record of the 1969 Eaglesham's Village Queen being crowned by the young Countess of Eglinton and Winton.

*   *   *

As they drove home, down past the old mill at Waterfoot, they saw several people wandering about the banks of the river and three cars parked on a low-walled enclosure just above the water.

114

"Have you any idea why that is laid out that way, Mum? Would it have been made solely for cars to park in?" Dianne asked.

"I often wondered about that myself, but only recently a man who was born and bred here told me its history. It used to be the site of an old cooper's house and it was a usual thing to see the works of his trade, things like buckets, tin baths for the before-the-fire bath ritual of past days, and washing boilers, lying around the little stone-built cottage. He lived alone, tho' whether he was a bachelor or widower seems uncertain, and kept an old gander which he called Cobbie. There is a tiny island where the Cart is joined by the Earn on which the old bird used to sit and snooze: the older he became, the more he enjoyed "his" island retreat, till it eventually derived the name of "Cobbie's Isle".

"You seem to hear a lot about Eaglesham and places," laughed Dianne. "How do you manage it?"

"I suppose when people find you are interested in any place they will tell you what they know about it."

"One of the decorated floats in the procession had an aeroplane on it. Do you know any story about that?"

"Yes, Lynne. During the war one of the German leaders flew here to try to make the British Government agree to terms with Germany. His name was Rudolph Hess and his 'plane crashed in a farmer's field just across there," Jo pointed vaguely towards pastoral land lying to their left. "I can remember the incident well; it was quite a sensation at the time."

"What was he doing up here if he wanted to see anyone in the Government?" Dianne's voice held more than a hint of scepticism.

"Apparently he had become acquainted with the 14th Duke of Hamilton at the 1936 Olympic Games (both were aviation-pioneers) and was under the false impression that as Scotland's premier duke he could go over the head of Britain's Prime Minister and agree to peace plans drawn up by Hitler, whose Deputy he was."

"Wait a minute, Mum. How come he was flying over Eaglesham? I thought the Duke of Hamilton's palace was where our College is right now."

"It was at one time, but I don't know when. I believe it was Dungavel Castle he was making for, but that he mistook the turrets of a mansion house here, known locally as the Castle, but really Eaglesham House, and crash-landed only a matter of a few hundred yards from it."

"It still doesn't make sense, though. Where is this Dungavel Castle and what about the Duke? Where does he come in?" Dianne was more puzzled than anything at the additional information.

"Dungavel Castle is near Muirkirk, I think between there and Strathaven, and was the Duke's lodge where Hess was once supposed to have stayed on a visit."

"Ah. That makes more sense."

"Dianne, did you know that Grandpa once lived in Eaglesham?"

"No. Did he, Mum? When he was a boy?"

"He was a married man with three of a family," Jo told them. "After he returned to Scotland from Australia, he brought your Gran and their three children to live in the village for a short time."

"So you are the only one in your family who didn't live there at all, yet you are the one who is most interested in it now!"

"Yes. I feel the same way about Australia, too, but I can't dot across there when I feel like it, the way I can do with Eaglesham," she laughed. "That's rather strange. As I said that, it dawned on me that Dot is across there."

"Dot who?"

"I honestly can't remember her surname."

"Well, who is she?"

"My cousin, Dorothy. Gosh! Isn't that awful, not even knowing her married name."

"I suppose you hardly know her. After all, you were only an infant when you visited your Australian relatives."

"She isn't one of them, though. She only went over there after she married. A few years after, in fact, because I remember her first son was only a few days older than you and our respective mothers used to discuss the progress of their respective almost-of-an-age grandchildren."

"You were quite well acquainted, then?"

"Certainly. We were good chums in our school days. I used to visit them a lot. They lived in a super old house, with three floors and a long, dark passage running beneath it which we children referred to as the 'secret passage'."

"Where did they live, then. Quite near you?"

"Not really very near. Nearer here, actually."

"Take us to see the house, Mum, please."

"I suppose I could, Lynne. It's just past this next junction."

"Has this junction a name?"

"They used to call it 'The Sheddons' but I don't know whether they still do."

"Don't you ever write to your cousin Dot?"

"I'm ashamed to say I never have. I must find out her address and drop a note asking how she likes life in Australia."

"Yes, you do that, Mum. I think I'd like to try Australia for myself. It would be good if I had someone there I could contact."

"Really, Dianne? Do you really mean you would go to Australia?" Her young sister never quite knew whether or not to believe everything the impetuous girl said.

"I do. Mum, what would you say if I did?"

"I really don't think I'd say anything against it; it's what I've always wanted to do myself, but your Dad isn't even interested. I still think I'd like to have a trip out before long, though."

"Why?"

"Lots of reasons, Lynne. I'd like to meet all those relatives I've only heard about or seen in photographs, as well as see the place my mother was born and where my sisters and brothers were born, too, for that matter. I've always felt I have more roots there than I have here, somehow."

As she spoke, she swung the big car into a side road.

"Is this where your cousin lived?"

"Yes, right down at the foot of the road. The very last house."

She drove the entire length of the Clarkston street and stopped the car outside the end house.

"That's the house—No. 44. Many a great time I had playing in the garden with my cousins."

"Where is the secret passage?"

"You had to enter it from the back garden. The bottom flat of the house had a door on a lower level, opening on to the back garden. The house belonged to my grandparents previously, and my grandfather made what had originally been a huge cellar area into additional bedrooms for my uncles, before they all married and left home. You should ask your own grandfather about the pranks they used to play in their days."

"I think I can understand what you must feel about wanting to see where your mother lived. You know about your father's people and where he lived, so you would like to compare that with the details of your mother's early life."

117

"That's just about it, Dianne."

"I tell you. Let's have a race, you and I, to find which of us will reach Australia first."

"Right, you're on."

"What about me?"

"Don't worry, Lynne. I won't forget about you?"

"Do you ever?" and Jo thought she detected a hint of jealousy in her elder daughter's tone.

Chapter 9

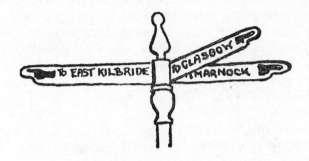

RENOWN

Within the next few years almost all the old properties had been either demolished or renovated. Those in the latter class had been restored as useful living accommodation in most cases. The gap sites left where old buildings had been completely demolished were quickly built upon, with strict adherence to the County Council's regulations. Properties which had housed many families a century ago were turned into single luxury homes for one family, a couple, or even single persons. Old stables, haystores, weaving sheds and even little cottages built on the ground at the back of the village houses, the roods of garden ground, as laid out on the original plan, were nearly all demolished.

With each visit she made to the village, Jo became more captivated. Ultimately, she approached the owner of about the last of the old places still in its original state, with regard to purchase. After somewhat prolonged transactions arrangements were drawn up for the sale and all that remained was to sign the legal documents. Without any warning the sale was called off by the seller.

The loss of the old property had come as a bitter disappointment to Jo, although her husband had no regrets; he had not altered his opinion of the village with the passing of the years.

One day during the early summer of 1971 Jo attended a "meet" of the National Trust in Eaglesham, at which more than a hundred

119

*members were present, including the Chairman and National Secretary.
On entering the village's public hall, Montgomerie Hall, somebody
mistook her for the Chairman's wife.*

*Jo's husband gave her the price of a return flight to Australia, and
sufficient to allow her to travel fairly extensively in that country during
the seven weeks of her visit. She saw for herself the country town which
her own forebears had helped establish, changing it in a relatively
short time from a swampy area in the midst of rugged bushland into
the fine rural township in New South Wales which is well known to the
country's many agriculturists. When there, she learned that her mother
had written graphic accounts of the little village in Scotland and told
the sisters whom she had left in Australia about its old houses and
interesting history.*

*Shortly after Jo's return, she formed part of a coach party which
toured the village by arrangement with the National Trust for Scotland.*

* * *

Each time Jo visited Eaglesham yet another of the old properties was
humming with tradesmen busily employed at restoring, renovating or
even rebuilding it.

She had never really put down any roots in the Cathcart house and
neither of the girls liked staying there very much, both feeling the
lack of company around their own ages.

Alex had been adamant in his refusal to be interested in Eaglesham's
old buildings, but Jo did her best to make him interested in its new
ones. They viewed one or two which had previously been occupied, but
there seemed to be something against them all. Then early in 1970 they
took out an option on a villa nearing completion by a local building
firm, and put their home on the market. It sold immediately, forcing
them to look for a house which they would be able to occupy at an
earlier date than the Eaglesham one. Jo was bitterly disappointed. So
near—and yet!

Every other day found her heading in her little car for the quiet
village tucked into a green corner of countryside at the foot of the
moors. Longingly she watched the tiny cottage homes of a past century
gradually emerge into lovely luxury houses for their new owners. Old
sheds which had been used to house livestock and fodder in the days
of their origin, then perhaps adapted at a later date to accommodate the

big wooden looms of the handloom weavers, were pulled down. Long back areas which had raised domestic crops or flax for weaving, were transformed into beautifully landscaped gardens, tasteful and secluded. Envy possessed her each time she walked up or down either of the main streets. Although she was comfortably installed in an almost new villa in a neighbouring village, something inside her craved for Eaglesham.

The new house there, on which they had the option before purchasing their present home, still stood empty. She wished they had settled for it instead.

She knew that Alex was displeased at her continuing obsession with Eaglesham, because he showed his disfavour at her persistent reference and constant visits to it, but she seemed unable to resist its captivating appeal.

Many hours she spent walking up and down the village's streets, peering at this, studying that, admiring the other, and many more hours were spent reading every available piece of writing connected to it.

A single-storey house in Montgomery Street always attracted her attention by its neat, compact appearance. In addition, the inscription over one of its windows never failed to stir her imagination, and she used to stand gazing at it while she conjured up pictures of its past owners.

On a particular occasion an elderly woman with a plump white dog watched her as she surveyed the little building. For a moment, Jo thought she was going to speak to her, then without warning she turned on her heel and crossed the grass in the Orry, the dog following leisurely.

One after another of the houses began to take fresh shape under the hand of their new owners, until there was scarcely one of the previously common sights—a boarded or derelict property—to be seen.

Then one sunny day in February of the following year she drove her coffee-and-cream-coloured Riley Elf up the familiar road yet again. She toured all around the ultra-modern new residences in course of erection on the hill behind Polnoon Street. She stood inside one of somewhat unusual design, wondering whether she could be happy living there, when she was joined by a woman rather younger than herself.

"This looks nice. I like the natural wood roof in this room."

"I was beginning to ask myself whether or not I did like it."

"Do you have any idea what the price is?"

"Yes. Here is the list."

"We have just motored up from England and are on our way to some estate agents in Glasgow. We had been told about this place, so we made for it first. My!"

Jo looked at the speaker's expression to determine the meaning of her ejaculation.

"The price?" she ventured.

"Yes, rather!"

"It is a bit steep, isn't it?"

"You think so? Help, no! It would be far, far more down south. I say, I think I'll go fetch my hubby."

Without further ado, she was off. Jo wandered leisurely about from room to room, still trying to make up her mind whether or not she really cared for its new-fangled interior. Then the peace was shattered. The young woman had returned complete with husband and four young children, all falling over themselves to investigate their mother's find.

"Excuse me, please. My wife tells me you have a price list for this property."

"Yes, I have."

"Does it give the builder's or the selling agent's address? She has fallen for it right off. We'll go right in to their office if you can tell me where it is."

Jo gasped! That was how to go about business. No hint of Scots canniness there, anyway. She laughed.

"My word. You are quick workers. Here, have this list. The name and address of the builders are at the foot."

The children were running all over the place, pulling at door handles, trying waterless taps, sliding the sliding doors and operating window catches. Their mother was already placing her furniture and choosing her colour schemes.

"Come on, Vicky. We'll go into Glasgow right away and settle for it."

Jo felt compelled to speak.

"I hope you don't think I'm cheeky, but don't you think you should wait until you have seen some other houses?"

The couple looked at her rather blankly, as though she had uttered some foolishness. She explained her reasoning.

"There are lots of new houses being built here—and even more on the north side of Glasgow. The builders are finding it slow to sell them.

122

We nearly bought a new one down the road, about a year ago, and it's still not sold yet."

They gave her an even funnier look, making her think that they judged she wasn't quite "all there". She gave up.

"We'll go and see these builders first, anyhow." Jo sighed, then took herself off, too.

She drove up Polnoon Street and turned down into Montgomery Street, stopping the car outside The Treasure Chest. After a browse through its treasures, old and not so old, she walked down to The Wishing Well. As usual, all the tables in the little teashop were piled with dainty home-made scones and cakes and all the chairs surrounding them were filled with leisured ladies and their escorts. The usual line up of cars decorated the street, both at the pavement side and along the green verge of the tree-lined Orry.

Deciding that she did not really wish to join the inevitable queue forming at the low doorway, she wandered down the street, meaning to return when the worst of the crush was over.

She drew level with an old building looking sadly out of keeping with its newly decorated neighbours. It was not by any means the first time she had noticed it, but this time she really studied it. The windows at waist level where whitened on the inside of the glass, but it was not difficult to see through the thin layer of white-wash.

Jo was intrigued at what she saw. The interior was a complete shambles. Bottles, old stools and chairs, an ancient fireplace and sink, and all the litter and accumulation of decades lay in profusion and carefree abandon throughout the whole area. The bare walls and crumbling ceiling complemented the scene and altogether it presented a compelling challenge to her.

Without ever stopping to consider her action, she rang the bell of the adjoining house and the door was opened by a cleaning woman. After only the briefest of pauses, Jo collected her thoughts and asked whether she could tell her the owner of the derelict house next door. After the woman had gone to see her mistress Jo took stock of the situation, but before many seconds, the other returned and invited her to join the lady of the house in a cup of tea.

After duly apologising for her intrusion, and being assured that the mistress was delighted to have some company, Jo was escorted into a delightful little parlour overlooking the grass of the Orry. She was given the information she desired and also shown over the house and garden of her hospitable hostess. Before she took her leave, the latter warned that if she had any sense she would have nothing to do "with that place next door".

Notwithstanding the well-meant and friendly advice, Jo hastily sought out the owner of the property which had beckoned her with such wondrous fascination. After some lengthy discussions, she agreed to buy it in its dilapidated state.

The large single room on the ground floor had been two different "single-end" houses originally and the upper portion, entered by an outside back stairway, had also been two separate houses. The old fireplaces, the food cupboards beside them, the recessed bed compartment, and the walk-in clothes closets adjoining them, were all still as they had been many, many years previously. Jo was totally carried away with its very antiquity.

The plans she had for the old property filled her thoughts all the way home and her spirits were high as she told Alex of it later. His initial lack of enthusiasm progressed to downright displeasure, but in spite of his unfavourable reaction, Jo proceeded with her plans to purchase.

One bright April day, when the deal was all but completed legally, she took four friends to see the old place. Their impressions of it varied.

"Goodness me! What a mess," said one as she peered through the grimy streaked whitewash on the windows at street level.

"You could make something of that, Jo," was the more hopeful comment of another as she studied the twisting stone stairway which rose from the back courtyard to the upper storey. "A glass wall encircling it and forming a sun lounge would be just lovely here."

"Yes, with climbing plants growing up the side of the stairs," one of the younger of them added.

"Watch your steps here," Jo warned as they all trooped up the narrow stairway which was crumbled away at parts. "Don't be tempted to hold the handrail, either, as it is liable to give way."

"I say, look at this." The youngest of them had entered the upper flat first and was surveying the contents of a cupboard. Rows of glass jars filled the top shelf, looking as though they had been there for decades. "Whatever is in these?" she queried.

"Looks like preserved fruit that has lost all its colour. Look at those, though!" Jo pointed to a dark corner of the cupboard. "Bats!" That had been enough for them all and they had taken a hurried leave of it.

Next day Jo visited the County Council offices in Paisley for advice on making alterations and improvements to it and staff there advised her about the ins and outs of buying the old property. She arranged with the County Engineer to meet at the Eaglesham address the following forenoon.

The morning dawned wet and cheerless and Jo parked her little car in its usual spot on the Mid Road. Walking up Montgomery Street in the rain, she wondered yet again how her own mother must have felt coming to the rural village. She spotted a van draw up outside the house she was buying and recognised its occupant as the gentleman from the Council. She had forewarned the owner of the property that the County Engineer's Department official would be meeting her on the spot to discuss the house.

"Good morning. We have both timed it well." She noted that he gave a distasteful look at the old property before replying.

"Yes, indeed. A dismal morning—and a dismal hole of a place, this." He made no effort to hide his disdain of the property.

Jo would not allow herself to be disenchanted.

"I'm told that it has lain empty for a very long time. I expect that it could be made quite nice."

"Well, I know it's many a long year since I first inspected it. It will take a mighty lot to make it look nice, I'll assure you."

Jo didn't want to be drawn into a discussion about its defects before they even entered its door, so declined to answer.

They were just drawing level with the door to the entry when the old man who was selling the house, stepped through the opening and joined them on the footpath.

"Good morning. You're ready waiting for us, I see."

Jo fully expected his tone to match her own in casual cheerfulness. It didn't.

"Morning." Then with a curt nod to her escort, "G'day. It's you, is it?"

The two men weighed each other up with their eyes. After a brief silence, he turned to Jo again.

"The deal's off."

She was so stunned that no words would come.

"I've decided that I'm not going to sell the old place."

In spite of herself, Jo couldn't stop the hot tears flooding her eyes. She was glad that her companion came to the rescue.

"What do you think you're going to do with it? You will never live in it."

"No, that I will not. I'm settled over there now. You ran me into some expense there."

"Well, you've a good house now, haven't you, so what are you worrying about?"

"Aye, but it cost me a pile of good money."

The younger man just shrugged his shoulders as though in dismissal of the subject.

Jo had regained some of her composure.

"We had arranged everything to our satisfaction, I thought. I even told your solicitor that I'd probably be back in to see him today, to sign up the legal documents."

"Yes, I know. You told me that yesterday."

Jo was completely nonplussed. She simply stood and stared at the old man's face. He seemed to feel ill at ease under her scrutiny and averted his gaze.

When she realised that no explanation was forthcoming she pressed for it.

"Can you tell me why you changed your mind?"

"I've decided to sell it together with the larger house adjoining it."

There was no gainsaying his right to do just that, but they had already discussed the whole position, on more than one occasion, and came to the conclusion that he would find it much easier to sell the "big house" without the derelict one next to it being part of the sale.

"Then there's nothing I can say to make you reconsider it?" She tried to make her voice sound hopeful, but knew that it had been a pretty poor attempt.

"I'm afraid not."

She looked searchingly into the ageing features and again detected his uneasiness under her penetrating look.

"Oh, well, I don't think the lady need worry very much. From what I remember, the place is falling to bits, anyway. Did you ever get that internal dampness put right?" the official note crept in.

After a few minutes more in conversation about the state of the property and the amount of money and work which would require to be expended on it, before it was at all presentable, the little group dispersed—the old man back through the entry doorway, the Council representative to the parked van and Jo down Montgomery Street.

Two or three weeks afterward the County Council's Planning Department exhibited plans and drawings of the village properties at a public meeting of the National Trust for Scotland. A picture of "her" property was prominent, with caption reading that it was one of the last requiring renovation. The sight of its sad appearance determined her on having at least one more try at buying the place.

After the meeting the party split into groups and were shown places of special interest by local guides. Jo felt that her group were fortunate in having a local architect, who shyly pointed out his own lovely home, as guide. He drew their attention to the inscription about the window of the cottage in Montgomery Street which Jo had often studied, telling them the owner was one of the ladies originally responsible for the preservation of the village.

Later that evening, Jo had walked past the inscribed lintel and caught a glimpse of quite a gathering of people within. Parked at the kerb was the large car which had followed her up the road to the village earlier, and which she had later learned conveyed the Marquis of Bute to the meeting in the Hall.

The next day she approached the old man again with regard to selling the property she wished to buy, and was again met with a refusal to sell it apart from the larger adjoining house. With exceeding reluctance, she was forced into giving up the project completely.

* * *

Alex had been quite pleased to learn that the deal had fallen through; he had never wanted her to have anything to do with the old property from the outset, she well knew, but his evident delight at her loss of it only made matters worse for her. The passing weeks did nothing to assuage her keen sense of disappointment. To have been so near to owning a little place of her own in the coveted village, then have it snatched from under her nose at the eleventh hour, was indeed bitter medicine.

Despite her disappointment she visited Eaglesham as often as she could throughout the ensuing months, still nursing her grievance.

Sitting beside the last glowing embers of the fire one late autumn evening, after both their daughters had gone upstairs to their bedrooms, Alex suggested she make a trip to Australia, promising to meet the fare and give her a generous amount of cash to spend during her stay.

127

"Do you really mean it?" She wasn't quite sure whether he was merely tormenting her or actually meaning what he said.

"Why not? You wanted me to spend more on a tumbledown old building to bury yourself away in, didn't you?"

"Oh, but I couldn't let you spend all that money on me."

"I'll tell you this much. I wouldn't spend it on anyone else."

Without further ado, it was arranged and soon she was flying in the first "Jumbo" Jet 'plane from London to Australia, preparing to find how her mother's native countryside compared with the land she had finished her life in—a thing she had often pondered.

"Well, Jo, what do you think of our Blue Mountains?"

The soft Australian drawl, as well as the gentle manner of the little white-haired lady, never failed to remind Jo of her own mother. She had wondered whether it would be easy to find her relatives here in this huge strange country of wonders. One look at the neatly dressed figure, standing on the platform of the quiet country station awaiting the arrival of the train, had been sufficient to tell her that the lady was undoubtedly "Mum's little sister".

Now she was seated across the lunch table from her, high up above the mountain ranges of New South Wales, in Katoomba's Skyway Restaurant. She took her time before answering, letting the circular revolving floor gently swing her around the dining-room so that her eyes could drink in more of the spectacular panorama confronting them through the huge windows.

Wide expanses of azure sky above low ranges of rock formation of a smokey midnight blue hue, provided a hypnotic backdrop for miles to the thickly-vegetated green gulleys far below. Standing starkly outlined by the midday sun's strong rays were the dramatic peaks of sandstone rock columns known as "The Three Sisters". Immediately prior to lunch, she and her cousin had been swaying in the cable car more than a thousand feet above the gorge-slashed Jamieson Valley, from which the rock columns rose. The view they had of the entire surrounding area, with its distinctive flora and unusual rock formation, amply compensated for any nervousness they may have felt in their swinging cabin. She had asked what gave the whole area its unique blueness and was told that it was the result of the oil exuding from the eucalyptus trees in the densely wooded valleys and deep gorges which bit into the spectacular sandstone precipices ringing the entire region. The oil

15. Looking over the Orry to the Church, today

16. Polnoon Street and the Orry, now

floats in the air in tiny droplets which refract light, producing the effect of making distant objects appear blue.

Now she thought again of the stunning impact which the very vastness of the scene, together with the vividness of nature's lighting effects, had created in her consciousness. She found it hard to express her thoughts but she knew that her aunt expected a reply.

"I think they are wonderful, just like everything else I've seen in Australia. I love it all. It's an entirely different world to the one I've come from."

"That's what your mother said about Scotland when she first went over there to live."

"Goodness. Did she think it was wonderful? I should have thought it would break her heart to leave all this behind and go to dirty Glasgow."

"I meant that she thought Scotland was an entirely different world to the one she had come from." Again the quiet dignified tone conjured up memories of her mother..

"Of course. It is, too."

"Did she speak much of Australia, Jo?"

"She did to me. I think it was because I was the youngest, as though she had to convey her inmost thoughts to the last of her children to carry on to posterity."

"I think I can understand that."

Jo looked across the table at her cousin, the youngest of her aunt's own family, then at her aunt.

"I'm sure you can. You remind me so strongly of her, Aunt Bessie."

The lined features of the older woman creased into a pleased smile and her eyes lit up.

"I take that as a compliment. Your mother was always greatly loved and respected."

"She deserved both." As Jo said it, she felt humbly grateful to have had such a mother.

"I certainly agree."

"Didn't you once tell me that Aunt Eileen and Uncle Tom spent their honeymoon in the Blue Mountains, Mum?"

"That's right. Not far from Katoomba."

"Must have been more than half a century ago. Before you or I were born, Jo."

"Long before." The cousins exchanged looks, then laughed at their own reticence.

"It does seem a long way back but I can remember it all so well." A far-away look crossed over the old lady's eyes and she sat silent for a long moment before continuing. "She was so happy in Sydney with her two little girls and even more so when her son was born. Then without warning she was whisked off to the other side of the globe to live in a strange land with people she had never met."

"Do you think she was very unhappy about it?"

"She used to try to convey her feelings in the letters she wrote me, but tried to hide them from our parents who didn't approve of the move at all. I know she was not at all happy when she first arrived, but I remember what a change there was in her letters when she moved into a little village."

"Can you remember the name of the village?" Jo was agog to learn if it was where she thought it might be.

"Oh, yes. It was called Eaglesham. I've never forgotten the name. Do you know it?"

"Very well. It is the neighbouring village to our own."

"How far away is that?"

"Near enough for me to see it clearly from my upstairs window." Jo laughed.

"As near as that?" Her cousin showed surprise.

"It seems strange to us to think you can see one village from another, but I expect neighbouring communities there are very much nearer than they are here."

"Very much so," Jo agreed.

"Eileen told us that Eaglesham was quite a historic place. She apparently found it very interesting and I remember she used to write about it at length in some of her letters."

"Yes. Its story goes back a long way. The present village was rebuilt slightly more than two hundred years ago, but there was a hamlet there for a long time before that, of course."

"Is there any of the original village left?"

"You mean the rebuilt one? Oh, yes. It's still all there today, though of course there have been a lot of changes."

"That means it was built before Captain Cook landed here! It's still lived in, then, is it?"

Jo had to laugh at her cousin's amazement.

"It certainly is. In fact it is quite a show piece for the district and houses in it are hard to come by."

"Are they proper homes, or just shacks?"

"My goodness, no. Some of them are certainly small cottages, but it also boasts some fair-sized houses, by Scottish standards, that is."

"It would be wonderful to see some of the old places in Great Britain," her aunt mused.

The use of the adjective reminded Jo that in her aunt's younger days all colonials probably thought of Britain as Great, just as the majority of them thought of it as their Motherland.

*   *   *

Jo enjoyed her time in Australia to the full and would gladly have stayed much longer, but duty awaited her at home.

During April of 1972, not long after her return, she and a colleague formed part of a coach party arranged by the National Trust for Scotland. The coaches, about fifteen of them, left from nearby East Kilbride and toured the area, both the new and the old parts.

Members of the Trust had come from all over Scotland to attend the Annual General Meeting which took place in the forenoon. Following lunch, most of them joined the coach tour which had been advertised as a tour of the old villages of Maxwellton and Eaglesham. Neither Jo nor her companion had expected such a large number.

"I didn't know that the Trust had so many enthusiasts, did you?"

"I certainly did not expect as many coaches as this." Jo looked over her shoulder to the long line of single-deck buses following.

"Eaglesham will certainly be busy when they all arrive."

In no time the long line of vehicles had driven up the hill in Montgomery Street and down the entire length of Polnoon Street, without stopping.

"Are we not being allowed off here?"

"I would like to see some of these little houses at closer range."

"What an unusual lay-out."

From all sides the comments of the occupants made it obvious that the village was of great interest.

"It seems a pity not to stop the buses and let the people have a look around." Jo was sure that practically all of them wished to do just that.

Her English companion for the day agreed wholeheartedly.

"But wouldn't it be difficult," he asked with a quiet chuckle, "if they all decided to have afternoon tea in the 'Wishing Well'?"

"It is amazing how many folk in different places have heard of Eaglesham. Do you know, my relatives out in Australia asked me about it. They had remembered my mother's mention of it years ago, in her letters home."

Chapter 10

TRANSFORMATION

The Tercentenary of the Act of Parliament which was passed in 1672, authorising a yearly fair and a weekly market, was celebrated in various ways and by several events. During the attendance of these Jo and her elder daughter visited some of the newer business premises in the village.

The younger woman, shortly expecting to leave Scotland for Australia, showed marked interest in the way the various proprietors tackled their many problems, and set about learning all she could of the ins and outs of such projects—thinking she might be able to emulate them at a future date and in another hemisphere. By arrangement, some of the people concerned showed her their premises and explained the handling of their business. In this way, it became evident that the new types of business had brought a new public to the village.

Conversations with some of the older residents revealed the fact that the newcomers were not altogether welcome. In spite of themselves, though, they had to admit that with their coming a new influx of prosperity had dawned. Just as the incomers of the nineteenth century had proved a somewhat mixed blessing, likewise these of the late twentieth century would prove. In the same way as the Industrial Revolution had brought economic changes to Eaglesham in the past, so *the Technical Revolution with its mobile population would bring at the present.*

Despite all the changes of the centuries, though, Eaglesham still managed to retain both its identity and its individuality.

A month after the Tercentenary Fair Jo's daughter took farewell of her parents, of Scotland her native heath, and of Eaglesham . . . and flew off to the sunshine in Australia.

* * *

By the tone of the letters she had written home, and the glowing accounts of life in Australia, which she had delivered to her household on returning, Jo had fired her elder daughter's imagination.

Within days of her mother's return, she made up her mind to go and try life over there for herself. The Australian Emigration Authority seemed eager to take a 21-year-old single girl, because within a couple of months all the routine forms and interviews were completed.

Early in May she received a telephone call from their London office asking her to forward her passport. Only then did the full impact of her decision appear to come home to her.

Jo had spent a few hours working in the garden and was clearing up her gardening tools when Dianne came home from the Bank where she was employed. Seeing her mother down at the foot of the garden, she walked round the side of the house and down the twisting path to the rockery.

"You have been busy as usual, I see. It's looking nice now, Mum."

"Yes, the little bit of sunshine has helped."

Jo thought her daughter looked unusually tired and pale.

"Have you had a busy day?"

"Not really. About the same as usual, I'd say."

Both studied the little rockery plants which were beginning to bloom, then Dianne suddenly dropped her shopper on the slabbed path and threw her arms upward and outward in an encircling gesture.

"My goodness! Physical jerks in the garden! Well, perhaps it's the 'in' thing, I wouldn't know!" Jo shrugged.

"Oh, Mum. This is how I'll always think of you when I am thousands of miles away. I'll see this garden with the rockery and the fish pond down at the bottom of it, and I'll think about that gorgeous laburnum tree in the middle of the lawn, just as it is now in full yellow dress, and my own wee Mum pottering among the plants."

"Don't you worry, my lady. You will have so many exciting new things to see out there that you will seldom spare a thought for the scenes you have left behind here."

"It's an awfully big step I am taking, is it not?"

"Certainly it is, but I give you credit for having weighed up the whole idea before you embarked on it."

"I don't know."

"Of course you did, you know that. You are just taking cold feet now because you have had something positive happening. For the past few months it has been more of an 'airy-fairy' idea than anything; now it shows signs of an imminent reality, that's all."

"I feel like a wee infant again, just as I felt one day at Annette Street school."

"Was that the day the teacher had to bring you home herself?"

"That's right. I can't remember her name but she was so kind and understanding when I told her I would be all right once I was with you."

"I remember it well. She had you by the hand and gently handed you, quite literally, over to me saying, 'Your little girl has an attack of "butterflies in her tummy" and the only person to cure that is her mother'."

"Oh, Mum. I feel just the same now, so do you think you can still cure 'butterflies'?"

"Run in and make a cup of coffee while I tidy up here and I'll have a cup with you. It will be a good hour before the others are home for tea."

As they sat drinking their coffee, Jo studied her daughter's expression in an attempt to penetrate her thoughts. She knew that it was the posting of the passport which had caused the misgivings but wondered whether there was more to it. Her daughter had been seeing a lot of a young man in one of the Bank's other branches and now Jo began to wonder if there was more to the friendship than the girl cared to admit.

"What does Ian think about your going to Australia?"

"He thinks I'm plain stupid, throwing away all my background and my present comforts here."

"Does that worry you? I mean the fact that he thinks that."

"Not in the slightest. He's entitled to think what he will, I don't care. It doesn't concern me what he or anyone else thinks, for that matter."

At least she has not formed any attachment there, Jo thought, or it surely would concern her.

"I think what really worries me is that you and Dad will be half a world away from me."

Jo felt that anything else she could have said would have been less of a shock than that. For years this girl of hers had been kicking for all she was worth against the parental authority which she and Alex had always believed to be but their duty to exert. Now when she was but a stone's throw away to complete freedom from it, she hesitated to grasp the longed-for emancipation.

"Don't try to pretend that will be a worry. It is exactly what you have wished for over a long period."

Dianne did not answer for a moment or two, but just sat looking into her coffee. When she did at last speak, it seemed to Jo that the words had to be pulled to the surface from a great way down in her consciousness.

"I suppose that I have wanted to shake you both off. But I honestly know that if ever I do, I won't be any use without you." She still did not lift her eyes, and in the long pause that followed both mother and daughter went back down the years in their thoughts.

"If you and Dad were not there as my rock to grab hold on, I know I would go under." Her voice was low and unusually quiet. Seldom did she give any opportunity for sensible or serious discussion. Jo grabbed at this one when she had the chance.

"You also know that when we are not present, a much better help is always available, wherever you may be in His universe."

There was no reply but Jo saw her girl blink away the quick tears which had spilled over, causing black eye-make-up to streak her finely chiselled features.

In spite of the seriousness of the moment, she wanted to smile at the comical picture Dianne presented. Instead, she rose and laid her arm lightly across the narrow shoulders.

"Come on, cheer up, hen." She subconsciously used her own mother's pet name for herself, which had never ceased to bring comfort when she had needed it. "Perhaps we'll all be out in sunny Aussie some day, you never know."

"Oh, Mum. I hope so."

"Come and help me prepare tea, will you. I want to go up to Eaglesham this evening."

Dianne laughed, and the tension broke.

"As always. Really, Mum, I'm sure your ghost will haunt that place!"

"So long as it enjoys it as much as I do, then that will be all right."

"Whatever do you find to do when you go there, anyway?"

"Well, there is plenty of activity these days."

"What kind of activity, though?"

"Art Exhibition, Ceilidh, Tennis Tournament, Concerts, Photo Exhibition. . . ."

"You must be kidding."

"Badminton and Bowling, Talks, oh and something in your line—the 'Messiah', or parts of it, is being performed in the Parish Church on Sunday night."

"Are you really serious?"

"Of course I am. Why shouldn't I be?"

"But Eaglesham! Surely a place that size doesn't have all those social events around the same time."

"It does just now, I assure you."

"Then is it a special occasion, or what?"

"Yes. It's their Tercentenary Celebrations."

"Of what?"

"The Royal Charter."

"Stop pulling my leg, Mum. As if a wee village like that could lay claim to any Royal Charter."

"I'm not kidding you and it was certainly granted one by King Charles II away back in 1672, when they were given authority to hold a weekly market and a yearly fair."

"I say! Then it's celebration time there these days, like it was a few years ago when we went to a fair and saw some duchess or other crowning the village queen. I remember you had Dad's camera and it wouldn't work for either of us. That was a giggle."

"Do you think so? It was a positive menace, I think. I wanted photos of that ceremony which, incidentally, was carried out by the Countess of Eglinton and Winton."

"Oh, well, I knew it was somebody with a handle to her name."

"Dianne!"

"Titles don't mean a thing nowadays, Mum." She flicked her slender fingers in the air as if to dismiss all such things. "They go for nothing in this new society."

"Those which have been handed down for centuries don't go for nothing."

"Well, never mind. None of us will ever have any. Maybe I'll come with you this evening: I've nothing arranged."

Jo was secretly amused at her daughter's condescension, but chose to hide her amusement.

As it turned out, Dianne accompanied her mother on several of her trips to Eaglesham during that particular period and became quite impressed with the little community. Before long, it had cast its peculiar spell on the grand-daughter of the Australian lady who had come to live there half a century before.

It was a very different Eaglesham to the one she had known, or at any rate the events taking place were different. The celebrations commemorating the 300th anniversary of the granting of the Royal Charter were preceded by another event. A memorial stone had been erected on the Orry, at the foot of Polnoon Street and near the junction with Gilmour Street, to commemorate the work done by certain individuals to ensure the village's conservation. An oak casket had been buried in the ground beneath the stone. Inside the casket were selected items relative to life in the village in 1972. Included were maps, photographs, newspaper, stamps, coins, and even a priced catalogue from a mail-order firm. The official unveiling of the Memorial was performed with due ceremony by the Marquess of Bute on the 7th May, the first Sunday of the Tercentenary Celebration period.

The local Scout Group—the 15th Glasgow (Eaglesham)—chose the following day as a fitting time to perform the Official Opening Ceremony of their Headquarters and invited a well-known figure in commerce, Sir Hugh Fraser, to officiate.

A local artist, Mr. Ronald Paton, graduate of Glasgow School of Art, executed an etching of Montgomery Street with the Parish Church prominently portrayed, and this was on sale as the Tercentenary Souvenir.

The school hall was packed with interested hearers and viewers when Renfrewshire's First District Clerk, Mr. George Thomson, presented an illustrated talk on the history of the village.

The Parish Church rang to the sound of voices from neighbouring churches as their members joined with some of its own members, in the rendering of Handel's famous music, when excerpts from "Messiah" were sung.

138

Children from other schools within the First District of Renfrewshire joined with Eaglesham school children in the display of paintings for the Children's Art Exhibition. Displays were also organised by various youth organisations and the primary school held an open night for visitors.

In fact, it seemed that with something out of the ordinary happening on every hand, Eaglesham had succeeded in catering for all tastes and age groups.

"Eaglesham Old and New"—a photographic exhibition shown in the Lesser Church Hall—was one of the favourite attractions, with its collection of old-time village views contrasted against corresponding present-day ones. Many were thrilled at the sight of long-forgotten faces and places and the men who had put so much effort into the copying of treasured family photographs must have found ample reward in seeing the pleasure their labours provided to so many ordinary folk.

Ordinary folk were what Eaglesham was made for and these people chose "Fair Time" to honour a well-loved figure in their midst, when they presented a gift collected by the local school children to the man who had kept the village's roads swept clean for years. He had also shown constant concern for the welfare of Eaglesham's children, who now acknowledged their debt at the time of his retiral. Such, thought Jo, is the quality of life in Eaglesham.

"The Fair" itself was the wind-up to the days of celebrating. A spectacular touch was lent to its official opening when a package was dropped from an aircraft flying low over the field, retrieved by a R.A.F. corporal and handed to the Lord Lieutenant of Renfrewshire, great-great-grandson of an Eaglesham blacksmith of yore, the Rt. Hon. Viscount Muirshiel, C.H., C.M.G., who had been Scotland's Secretary of State when Eaglesham was listed as being of architectural and historic interest.

The package contained a photostat copy of Eaglesham's own Act of Parliament (Scots), obtained by Alexander, eighth Earl of Eglinton, on 21st August 1672 which granted "ane yeirlie frie fair to be keepit within the kirktoun of Eglishame upon the twentie fourt day of Aprile yeirlie with ane weekly mercat to be kept therat upon each Thursday, for buying and selling of all sort of merchandise and other commodities necessar and useful for the country".

The "Kilmarnock Bunnet" race was inaugurated at the time of the original granting of the Charter for the Fair. It was undertaken both on horseback and on foot but the mounted part was discontinued in 1860, being considered too dangerous. The race had been run at Eaglesham Fair Days ever since its inauguration and the prize was "a large Kilmarnock Coronet gaily decorated with ribbons which had adorned the cranium of the oldest Feuar in the Parade". Appropriately, the winner of the Tercentenary Fair race had newly been signed up by Kilmarnock Football Club.

After Jo and Dianne had seen all they wished of the Fair activities, they took a leisurely walk all around the village. The weather had managed to stay "fair for the Fair" and most of the residents were still at the scenes of the festivities.

"That's a bit of an eyesore on the corner there," remarked Dianne as she looked towards the foot of Polnoon Street. "Why has no one bought those old houses, I wonder."

"They are not for sale. They belong to the S.C.W.S.—I asked about them long ago."

"Of course! I should have known," she laughed.

"They have been lying empty for about two years now. When I asked at the Property Department of the Co-op what was to happen to them I was told that several proposals were under consideration which their architects were presently working on. They must have thought I represented a local committee, I think, because they hastened to add that the Preservation Society wishes would be given consideration."

"Let's take a look at them, Mum."

Together Jo and Dianne entered one of the old "Closes" and walked through the narrow entry to the back of the building which formed the corner of Polnoon Street and Gilmour Street.

The entire back area presented a scene of neglect which, when added to the desolate appearance of the actual building with its uncurtained windows and unlived-in atmosphere, appalled them. Nothing could have been more different to the beautifully restored houses elsewhere in the village.

Each looked about unbelievingly. Dianne was the first to speak.

"There's an open door in the corner. I'm going to have a look inside."

Without further hesitation, she ran up the flight of rough stone steps which led to the narrow iron-railed platform on to which the upper flatted dwellings opened. Jo followed more leisurely, noticing that the railings which flanked the stairway and continued along the front of the landing were the simplest and most unadorned which she had ever seen.

When she joined Dianne inside the house she found the girl deep in thought. They stood in what had been the kitchen, a room no more than about twelve feet by fifteen feet with a small sink (boasting only a single tap) fitted under the narrow window, and an old blue-tiled kitchen range complete with side oven, soot box, and metal front, practically filled one side of the room.

Without speaking, she walked into the only other apartment of the tiny house and she heard her daughter's footsteps follow her in. Although this was obviously the main room, it was not much bigger— about fifteen feet by twenty feet—but it did have recesses in one wall.

"Would this be for a single person?" Dianne's voice held a puzzled note.

"It wouldn't be built for such, if that's what you mean. This was an average family home for a working man."

"Where did they go, though?"

"They didn't go . . . they stayed, right here."

"There's no bedrooms and not a bathroom, either."

Jo explained to the perplexed girl that the recessed wall in the front room probably housed two inset beds with a dividing wall between, and that the parents more than likely slept on a bed tucked into a corner of the kitchen.

"It must have been awful; cooking, eating, washing, sleeping—all in the one little room. What must the atmosphere have been like?"

"The most comforting I've ever experienced. Your Gran and Grandpa had a little house like this in Largs, which they used as a holiday house. I can remember how good I used to feel when I was allowed to sleep in 'the kitchen bed' beside by mother on the rare occasions when my father was not staying there. Being the youngest by several years, I had to go to bed earlier than the others. I used to be made to face the wall so that the light from the gas bracket above the big high mantelpiece of the range did not keep me awake. I did lie awake, though, for as long as I could, savouring the comfortable glow of a happy family atmosphere. There was always a bright coal fire burning in the highly-polished range which had two square boxes fitted to the corners of its "fender" or kerb. One acted as a slipper box and the other as a log

141

box, into which we used to empty pockets-full of fir cones collected on our rambles. We used to vie with one another for the chance to sit on the padded hinged lids of these boxes, which made cosy fireside stools. As I lay in bed with a sheet covering my eyes I listened to the happy crackling of the coal and driftwood or cones as they burned in the grate, to the peculiar hissing noise from the gas mantle as it shed its incandescent light throughout the kitchen, and to the gay chatter of my brother and sisters."

"What about your mother? What would Gran be doing?"

"Very often she would be over at the sink, washing our clothes for us to dirty all over again as we played on the shingly beach or at the oily boats for hire. Or she would be ironing at the scrubbed table, using a weird-looking tall handiron which was operated by gas, or an assortment of smaller flat irons made of black cast iron, which she heated on an attachment to the firebars of the range."

"But didn't the place smell?"

"Oh, yes. Deliciously! With a mixture of hot soap suds, freshly laundered linen airing on the long wooden pulleys suspended from the ceiling, gas lighting, burning logs or fir cones, and most delectable of all—fresh bread toasting on the shining brass rack which swivelled across the redhot coals at the base of the firebox."

"Didn't you feel hungry, lying there smelling that?"

"Did I not? When I heard the butter being spread on the toast I used to drool at the mouth. Noises in the kitchen were so homely, too, but that noise often proved irresistible. I just had to endure a mild rebuke for not being asleep, by asking for some toast to eat in bed. It was delicious—sitting up in the 'hole-in-the-wall' bed, watching the others round the fire, and relishing every mouthful of the hot-buttered toast to protract the reprieve of the awaited order to 'settle down and get to sleep'."

"Yes, but was the sheer novelty of the situation not really a large part of its charm?"

"You could be right, but not entirely, I'm sure."

"Then there was the lack of bathrooms. Where did you bath, or even wash?"

"We took it in turns to wash at the sink, with water from the big iron kettle which always sat heating on the side of the range. Baths were nightly affairs, when the table had to be pushed back against the built-in coal bunker-cum-dresser to make room for the big zinc tub (housed under the recessed bed during the day) to sit in front of the blazing fire. Better by far than shivering in a cold tile-clad bathroom."

"Oh, come on, Mum. Distance is lending enchantment."

With that Dianne turned on her heel and delicately picked her dainty sandalled feet over the debris which lay scattered across the floorboards. She stood on the narrow outdoor landing for a moment, then turned towards the crude brickbuilt aperture astride its far end and sticking out from the main wall like an afterthought—and a sore thumb.

"That tiny cubicle, which can't be much more than four feet square, was the only toilet?"

"Yes, to serve several families."

"Oh, no, Mum. You can't tell me folks were better, nor the atmosphere more homely, living under such poor conditions. I wouldn't change places, anyway."

As she listened, Jo remembered expressing almost exactly the same sentiments to her parents many years before, when they had been discussing the old days in Eaglesham.

"We'll have a look at one more of the old places before we head for home, will we? Perhaps you're right, Dianne. The memories of child-hood are often enchanted, especially when one was blessed with a wonderful mother."

The next house they entered was sadly eloquent. It opened on to a tiny compartment which housed only a combined wooden coalbunker and potpress. The entire wall space above it was filled with heavy shelves, the underside of each having a row of cuphooks screwed into it. Facing that was the main door to the house, made of crude but solid wood, which opened on to the uncovered balcony or "landing" which extended along the length of the building. A row of coathooks was fitted on the back of the door and it had a deep shelf above it.

They walked through the kitchen into the larger room and both caught their breaths. Before them was a graphic lesson. An upright piano, in walnut with inset decorations and brass candlesticks, sat against one wall. On a table nearby was an invalid's rubber ring, token of someone's thoughtful care for a loved one. An old crude stool had been neatly covered with curtain material, while a square card table had been carefully enamelled and its top covered in an imitation marble finish. Parquet-type lino formed a surround to a flower-patterned waxcloth square. Thrift and poverty had marched hand in hand with tidiness and aspiration. Then the vandals came—smashing the piano, ripping the curtain cover on the stool, pulling a leg from the table and cutting great gashes in the rubber ring—for nothing better than the sheer "fun" of it all.

Sadly and thoughtfully they closed the door behind them and walked out into the sunshine again.

*   *   *

"Well, I'm glad I came with you, Mum. I really enjoyed all that."

Dianne sounded so surprised that Jo could not help but laugh at the remark.

"What's so funny?"

"Just what you said. Or at least, how you said it. As though you hadn't expected to enjoy yourself when you set out."

"Well, I didn't. Let's face it—it's not quite my scene, is it? I only came today, as I did the other evening, because I had nothing better to do."

"You are so nice!"

"Sorry, I didn't mean it that way. Oh, you know what I mean, Mum. A girl of twenty-one doesn't go around with her mother."

"Not if she can avoid it, I know. I didn't either, so don't worry. Never mind, you might be glad to remember that you did, when you are miles away."

Silence prevailed for a little and Jo was aware that her daughter was observing everything she saw from the car window.

"Is Australian countryside very different to all this? I hope I don't miss this too much."

"It is different, yes, but much more pleasant than I had imagined, especially around Melbourne where you are going."

"Then perhaps it won't be so bad. I love trees and things, though I never knew I did until quite recently.

"Be sure to visit my cousins in Berwick and Williamstown and in Dandenong, too. That's where your Grandpa's brother is as well. They will all make you very welcome."

"They were really good to you, weren't they? Which one had the swimming pool in the garden?"

"That's Dot. She lives in Berwick, a lovely rural little place. You'll like it there and she has written saying that you must treat it as your second home."

"Considering that she has never set eyes on me, I guess that's jolly decent of her. Is Berwick like Eaglesham?"

"Not quite! Though it has a kind of village quality which I liked. There was a lovely little spot not very far from it called Upper Beacons-field. I liked it, too. In fact, I took a photograph of the tiny church there, only to find there was no film in your Dad's camera, tho' he said there was!"

Dianne laughed heartily when she recalled that it was the same camera which had failed to operate in Eaglesham. "Then there is an affinity with Eaglesham after all."

"I suppose you could call it that. If I ever went out to Victoria to live, I think I would choose Upper Beaconsfield for my home. It is not nearly developed yet, but one day it will be quite a place. In fact, Dot and I used to discuss the possibility of going into partnership and setting up business there."

"It came as a big disappointment to you when Dad was promoted again, didn't it, Mum?"

"Yes, it did. I'm afraid I am a very selfish wife. Anyone else would be delighted to see her husband advance in his chosen career."

"I think it was because it came as such an anti-climax, really; there we were, sitting round the table after our first meal together only three hours after meeting you at the airport, wasn't it, when the 'phone rang. I'll never forget your face when you heard the news."

"Don't worry. I'll never forget the feeling. I had just been 'laying forth' about the marvellous opportunities in Australia and the advisa-bility of going out there, when I learned that your Dad was to be promoted to a higher rank. He had previously told me that if he ever was, he had no intention of changing employment—let alone country."

"Never mind. If I decide to settle over there, you can come and stay with me. Perhaps I'll buy a little business like the ones in Eaglesham. From what I've seen there recently, the small shop owners do not do too badly."

"The present ones do, but the previous ones had to shut down for want of business."

"Why should that have happened?"

"Largely because the shops were previously concerned with the sale of everyday commodities, from loaves of bread to packets of darning needles almost, and the growth of supermarkets within near reach has killed their trade."

"Are there none of that type of shop left now?"

"Not really. The present shops are rather specialised and, of course, cater for visitors as much as residents."

"They still do a good trade, though."

"True, because Eaglesham is something of an attraction now. Think of the visitors on a sunny week-end."

"How far is the little place you mentioned from Melbourne? Would city folk visit it on a week-end drive?"

"It must be between thirty and forty miles, which is not far in a country as vast as Australia, of course. Though whether people would choose it as a place to visit, when they have miles of sandy beaches on their doorsteps, is a more important factor."

"Mm! It would be nice to have something like the little fashion shop in the village, tucked away through the archway near Eaglesham church. Didn't you try to buy that cottage, Mum?" Dianne had been tormenting her and was surprised when she had answered.

"That and several others besides. I also considered a disused baker's shop with large bakehouse at the back and a smaller shop near the church. Both now serve as gift shops, as you know."

"I can just see you fitting in to either beautifully. What a pity you never succeeded in any of your projects. Poor old Mum; one of these days, you'll win!"

"An antique shop like 'The Treasure Chest' would do well in Australia, Dianne."

"I like 'The Wishing Well' better. Didn't you try to buy it?"

"Now you are teasing! I didn't, for the simple reason that it was sold before I heard about it being for sale. It was my aunt who told me about it opening up as a tea room. She knew the lady who had bought it and asked me, and your Aunt Jane and Aunt Anna, to patronise it. Now we can hardly get a seat in it."

"It's the same whenever you go, too. I've been up in the evenings sometimes and it's just as busy."

"Oh, have you. I didn't think Eaglesham was your scene!"

"It wasn't. I seem to be changing my tastes. Funnily enough, those I've introduced Eaglesham to seem to like it well enough."

"Mostly male, I suppose."

"Naturally."

"H'm."

"Yes, I think that's the kind of place I would like to start up in. How do you think that would go in Aussie, then?"

"In places where I tried to buy snacks on Saturday afternoons without any success, I'd say it would go like a bomb."

"Then I'll start baking again as soon as I get out there. I expect the lady who has 'The Wishing Well' is a fully trained professional, but never mind."

"She is not, you know. She just likes baking. In fact, when she first thought of buying that little place she envisaged it as a kind of open-door house."

"What do you mean?"

"She expected just the odd person or so to call in for a cup of tea now and again. In fact, she told me that she imagined she would be working away in her own part of the house, and when the bell rang on the opening of the door to the front street, she would stop what she was doing and make a pot of tea."

"Gosh. Think how different it has turned out."

"That's it. Well, here we are—home again."

"Now you'll have to make tea for your family, Mum, instead of for customers, like they do in Eaglesham."

*   *   *

The days sped into weeks and Dianne's plans proceeded apace. As the day of her departure loomed near, ever so many last-minute jobs cropped up, keeping both herself and Jo constantly on the move. The constant activity helped them keep their minds occupied, averting any long periods of waiting which could have resulted in the unpleasantness of second thoughts.

Only once did Jo's spirits plunge to the depths at the thought of letting her daughter go—and go so far. More than once, when the impetuous girl had attempted to leave home because of her parents' firmness, Jo had gone after her and brought her back. Now she was making no move to stop her going across the entire face of the globe, unaccompanied and unprotected.

The enormity of the undertaking hit her one evening when she was attending a party. Several of those present became the worse for drink, which always appalled Jo, and memories of her daughter's student days flooded into her mind. Fear gripped her heart, as she thought of what

147

might happen to the girl landed alone, or almost so, in a strange country and eager for every new experience she could grasp. No restraining hand or heart would be present then.

Panic-stricken, Jo left the party with the most hurried excuse she could muster up, and jumped into her old Riley Elf. She headed it out to the little cemetery near the old Mearns Kirk, over the moor from Eaglesham, without really being conscious of her motive. It was a fine night, and the big iron gate into the cemetery was not locked. Caring nothing for the party finery which she wore, she knelt on the ground in front of the granite memorial on her mother's grave, silently thanking

her Maker for the good woman who had brought her up to shun the evils so often encountered in life. Then she rose silently and in the full light of the moon, also rising, she placed her hand on the cool head-stone, as though drawing strength from the poor remains of the little Australian woman whose name it proudly bore. After a brief time thus, the turmoil in her soul subsided and with a deep inner peace she turned heart and head heavenward, asking God to help her wee lass as she set off to her own dear mother's land.

A few days later, the little party of father, mother, and sister drove with Dianne to the airport to bid her "Farewell" as she left them. Although the bulk of her luggage had gone on ahead, she still had an outsize suitcase as well as the usual amount of hand baggage.

Jo sought to help by carrying the heavy case but her daughter rebuffed her, saying as she would need to carry it herself for the rest of the journey, she would prefer to do so right away. Jo's heart sank. She was such a forlorn, lost-looking little lass, struggling alone under the weight of the case, and trying so hard to appear sure of knowing she was doing the right thing by going. And fooling none of them.

As the B.E.A. Trident aircraft slowly lifted from the tarmac of Glasgow Airport and flew off far, far into the mid-day sun, Jo felt that her heart would surely break. She watched it until the form of the plane was no more than a distant speck in the far horizon, then turned to join her husband and younger daughter on their way out to the car-park, each with the same thought uppermost in mind "What of her future?".

Chapter 11

DESTINY

Jo's cousin, who had promised to take a motherly interest in Dianne when she reached Australia, sent her son to Melbourne's Tullamarine airport with a car to meet the young Scotswoman. The instantaneous mutual attraction which the young couple experienced, very soon grew into a stronger and deeper feeling.

After a whirlwind courtship and before the onlookers could find their breath, wedding invitations were being despatched and preparations were being undertaken in all the usual ways. Dianne had hoped that her sister and parents would make the long journey to Australia to attend her wedding, but after consideration it was decided that they would postpone the trip until the newly-weds had settled into a home of their own.

Jo, especially, had felt very distant from her "little girl" at the time of the marriage, but when letters, photographs, tape recordings and the like began to arrive by post, she felt more a part of it all.

She had shown the photographs and played the tape recording to her father one day when he had paid them a short visit. Tears flowed unchecked as he sat with bowed head, listening to his own grand-daughter and his brother's grandson exchanging marriage vows. The years rolled back for Tom as he recalled the day when he had married Eileen in Australia. "Your mother said the very same words," he had falteringly told Jo, referring to the form of the wedding service.

Within months, the young people were delightedly writing Jo and Alex of the preparations they were making on the piece of land they had bought and the commencement of builders on the house which would soon be erected on it. The site they had chosen was in the very place Jo had told Dianne she would choose to stay in, if ever she took up residence in Victoria, and where the girl herself had light-heartedly replied would be her choice if she set up in business, like the shop-keepers of Eaglesham.

As she read all about the "stop-go" progress of the builders in one of Dianne's regular blue Aerogramme letter forms one day, it was Jo's turn to let the years roll back as she recalled her daughter's recent past.

All the concern which the girl had caused to her father and herself, seemed now to be like a particularly bad nightmare to Jo. The past was over, though she doubted if it would ever cease to play its part, and the future stretched invitingly ahead. What did it hold for them, she wondered, and especially for Dianne.

*　　*　　*

As Jo climbed upstairs to bed one glorious evening in early September her attention was caught by the colourful scene enclosed, like a painted landscape, by the staircase window frame. The setting sun's rays bathed the surrounding countryside in fiery tones and the new houses of Eaglesham glinted in its light.

She paused at the turn of the stair, resting her elbows on the wooden sill and her chin in her cupped hands, to survey the picture nature had created. As she gazed towards Eaglesham's church spire outlined against the glowing sky, she thought how strange it was that her mother had come to this very locality from far-off Australia and her daughter had left it to travel the same journey in the opposite direction.

151

In the warm light Eaglesham appeared rosy and Jo felt that was like a prophecy. With an inner glow which matched that of the sky, she contemplated that her daughter's future in Eileen's beloved land looked every bit as rosy.

APPENDIX

The Parish Church Register
of Eaglesham

No.	NAME OF COMMUNICANT.	PLACE OF RESIDENCE.	Profession, Occupation, or Designation.	Admission. For First Time Month. Da
				18
✓241	Mrs Robertson	North Side		
✓242	William Liddle	Backrow		
✓243	Mrs W. Liddle	Do		1862
✓244	John Hamilton	Backrow	Weaver	Dec
245	Adam Murray	North Side	Spinner	"
246	Irine Hall	Gilmour St		"
247	Thomas Kidney	Cheapside	Engraver	"
248	Mrs T. Kidney	Do		
✓249	Thomas McKay	Eaglesham House	Coachman	
✓250	Mrs T. McKay			
✓251	Mrs Archd Gall	Park		
✓252	George Gall	"		
✓253	Jane Whyte	Eaglesham House	Servant	
✓254	Isabella Denholm	"	Do	
✓255	David Shephard	"		
✓256	Mrs Margt Shephard	"		
✓257	Margaret Boyd		Servant	
✓258	John Robertson	Eaglesham House	Butler	1863
✓259	Alexr Melville	Backrow	Mason	Dec
✓260	Mrs A Melville	Do		"
✓261	Janet Melville	Do		"
262	Janet Picken	Revoch		"
✓263	Agnes Gall	Park		"
✓264	Grace Paterson	Woodhouse		"
✓265	Janet Young	Gilmour St		"
266	Jane Kennedy	Do		"
267	Jane Brown	Polnoon St		"
✓268	Jane Simpson	Townfoot		"
269	Jane Buchanan	Montgomery St		"
✓270	James Wilson			"

No. Day.	Admission by Certificate.		Disjoined by Certificate.		Removed by Death.		REMARKS.
	Place and Certifier.	When. Month Day.	Where Certified to.		Month.	Day.	
		1863			18		
							Left
		1863	Australia				Left
861	Mearns Rev. D. McKellar	Nov 9	Helensburgh				
	Do	Nov 9	Do				
	St Columba	May 14	Glasgow				
.8	Barony, Glas. Jas Struther	Dec 12	Hamilton				
4	Paisley Rev Alex Rennie	Nov 11	Keith				
	Do	Nov 11	"				
14	Falkirk Rev Will Begg 1863	24	Mary Hill				
17	Mearns Rev. D. McKellar						
			Camonstie				
		1864 Nov 11	Fintry				

No.	NAME OF COMMUNICANT.	PLACE OF RESIDENCE.	Profession, Occupation, or Designation.	Admission. For First Ti Month. D
				1863
271	James Scott	Polnoon St	Mason	Dec. 2
272	Mrs J. Scott	"		"
273	Barbara Young	"		"
274	Alice Bannister	Cheapside		"
275	Rosanna Muir			"
276	James Philp	Backrow	Land Steward
277	Mrs J. Philp	Do	
278	Ann Philp	Do	
279	Catherine McFarlane		
280	John McNaughton	Polnoon St	Constable
281	Mrs J. McNaughton	"	
282	James Brown	"	Baker
283	Mrs J. Brown	"	
284	Jane Gilmour	Reading room	
285	Arthur Yuill	Cheapside	Draper
286	Ann Rae	School House	Servant
287	William Dickson	Townfoot	Ploughman
288	Mrs W. Dickson	"	
289	Henry Stewart	Netherton	Shepherd	1864 Dec.
290	Mrs H. Stewart	"	
291	Hugh Fleming	Threepland	
292	John Smith	Borland	
293	Jane Smith		
294	John McIntyre		
295	Mrs J. McIntyre (Mary)		
296	William Fair		
297	Mrs Fair (Janet)		
298	Catherine McGilvray		
299	Wm McQueen		
300	Lilias McQueen		

Day.	Admission by Certificate.		Disjoined by Certificate.		Removed by Death.		REMARKS.
	Place and Certifier.	When. Month. Day.		Where Certified to.	Month. Day.		
		18			18		
	Hutchesontown						
	"						
	"						
	Mid Ch. Paisley	Octob. 25	Belfast				
	"	" "	"				
	Stranraer		Carronstie				
	"		"				
	Lauriestone						
	E. Kilbride						
25	Hamilton Free						
8	Mearns						
"	"		"				

No.		NAME OF COMMUNICANT.	PLACE OF RESIDENCE.	Profession, Occupation, or Designation.	Admission For First Month.
		G.			18
	1	Gilmour, Allan	Eaglesham House	Sole Heritor	
	2	Gilmour, Mrs			
1	3	Gilmour, Andrew	North Side	Carter	
2	4	Gilmour, Jane 2	Reading room		
3	5	Gemmell, Peter 3	South Side	Publican	
4	6	Gemmell, Mrs 4			
	7	Gardiner, John 5	South Side	Spinner	
	8	Gardiner, Mrs 6			
	9	Gavin, Mrs	Millhall		
5	10	Gavin, Ludovic 7	"	Manufacturer	
6	11	Gavin, Hugh 8	"	"	
7	12	Gray, Charles 9	South Side	Baker	
8	13	Gray, Mrs 10	"		
9	14	Gall, Mrs	Park		
10	15	Gall, George	"		
11	16	Gall, Agnes	"		
12	17	Govan, Mary (Mrs Young) 11	Nether Enoch		
13	18	Gardiner, John			21 Jun.
14	19	Gardiner, Mrs			21 June
15	20	Gilmour Mrs Andw 12			
16		Gardiner, Helen			
17		Gemmell, John 13			
18		Gemmell Mary 14			
19		Gemmell John			
20		Gordon Robt			
21		Gordon Mrs Robt			
		Gray Nancy 15			
		Geddes Mrs Robt 16			
		Granger David 17			
		Do Mrs 18			

Church

Dated.	Admission by Certificate.		Disjoined by Certificate.		Removed by Death.		REMARKS.
... Day.	Place and Certifier.	When. Month Day.	Where Certified to.	Month. Day.			
		18		18			
5	Dumbarton And Gray mint						

COMMUNICANTS' ROLL BOOK, for the

No.	NAME OF COMMUNICANT.	PLACE OF RESIDENCE.	Profession, Occupation, or Designation.	Admission. For First Time. Month. Da
				18
1.	Ludovic Gavin.	Millhall	Mill Owner	
2.	Mrs Janet Gavin.	"		
3.	Ludovic Gavin. Jun.	"		
4.	Hugh Gavin.	"		
5.	John Arneil	Cronkeys	Innkeeper & Postmaster	
6.	Mrs Arneil	"		
7.	Margaret Arneil.	"		
8.	Mary Arneil	"		
9.	Mrs Robt (Craig) Arneil.	South Side. Eaglesham.	Grocer.	
10.	Anna Arneil.	"		
11.	Allan Gilmour.	Eaglesham House.	Sole Heritor.	
12.	Mrs Isabella Gilmour	"		
13.	Mrs Gilmour.	Polnoon Lodge.		
14.	Isabella Gilmour.	"		
15.	Helen Gilmour.	"		
16.	William Howie.	Cheapside.		
17.	Marion B Howie.	"		
18.	Lizzie Howie.	"		
19.	Margt Howie.	"		
20.	Mary Howie.	"		
21.	John Wallace.	Cheapside	Labourer. Elder.	
22.	Mrs Wallace.	"		
23.	Margaret Wallace.	"		
24.	Margaret Hodgson.	Cheapside.		
25.	James Boyle Yuille	Schoolhouse.	Parochial Schoolmaster Elder.	
26.	Mrs J.B. Yuille.	"		
27.	James Begg.	Back row.	Blacksmith. Elder.	
28.	Mrs Begg.	" "		
29.	Andrew Yuille.	Cheapside	Grocer.	
30.	Mrs Yuille.	"		

ad. Day.	Admission by Certificate.		Disjoined by Certificate.			Removed by Death.		REMARKS.
	Place and Certifier.	When. Month	Day.	Where Certified to.		Month.	Day.	
		18				18		
		1862. Dec 15		St Luke's Glasgow.				
		1862 Oct 18		Glasgow				
						1862		
		1861		India.				
		1863 Oct	20	Bothwell				
		1863 Oct	20	Bothwell				
		Do		Do				

No.	NAME OF COMMUNICANT.	PLACE OF RESIDENCE.	Profession, Occupation, or Designation.	Admission. For First Time Month. D
61	William Wilson.	Lochcraig.	Farmer.	18
62	Mrs Wilson.	,,		
63	Eliza Wilson.	.		
64	James Fleming.	Windhill.	Farmer.	
65.	Mrs Fleming.	,,	-	
66.	John Scott.	Rivoch	Farmer	
67.	Mrs Scott.			
68.	James Stewart.	Cunat	Farmer.	
69	Mrs Stewart.	.		
70	Thomas Prentice.	Ardoch.	Farmer.	
71.	Mrs Prentice.	-		
72.	James Prentice.	.		
73.	Isabella Prentice.	.		
74.	Alexander Prentice.	Enoch Lodge.	Farmer.	
75.	Mrs Agnes H. Prentice.	,,		
76	James Young.	Enoch	Farmer.	
77.	Mrs Ann Young.	,,		
78	James Young.	.		
79	Alexander Young.	,,		
80	Margaret Young.	,,		
81	Mrs Mark Jean Young.	,,		
82	Mrs Robert Young.	Lowhill.	Farmer.	
83	Agnes Young.	.		
84	Janet Young.	.		
85	Peter Taylor.	Blackwood Hill.	Shepherd.	
86	Robert Hamilton.	Cheapside.		
87	Mrs Hamilton.	.		
88	Janet Hamilton.	.		
89	Lilias Hamilton.	-		
90	Helen Hamilton.	North Side.	Washerwoman.	

Parish Church of Eaglesham

Dated. Month. Day.	Admission by Certificate. Place and Certifier.	Disjoined by Certificate. When. Month Day.	Where Certified to.	Removed by Death. Month. Day.	REMARKS.
		18		18	
nov 1860.	U.P. Ch. of Eaglesham. Rev. Mr. Cornwall				
					Dead.
an 1859.	S. Kilbride. Rev. W. Carrick.				

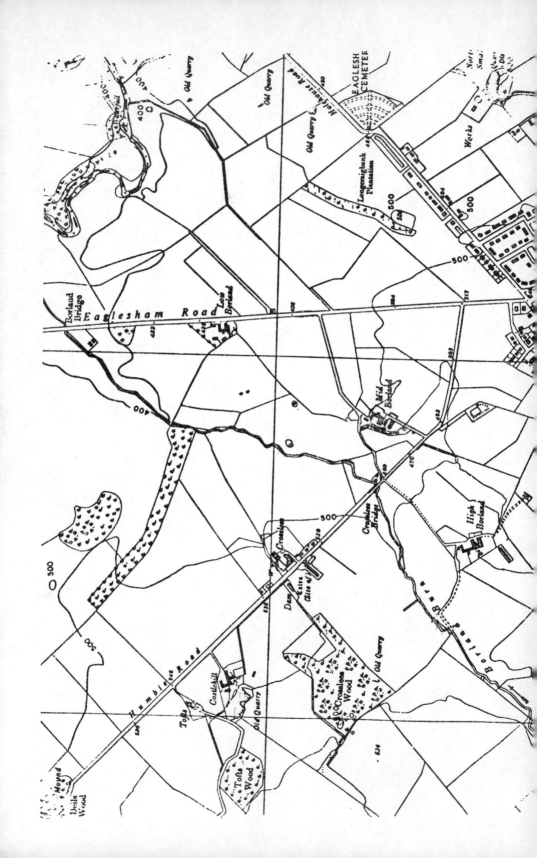